The Birdwatcher's Book of Lists

The Birdwatcher's Book of Lists

LISTS FOR RECREATION AND RECORDKEEPING

DR. LESTER L. SHORT

Curator, Department of Ornithology
American Museum of Natural History

Illustrations by

JUAN LUIS G. VELA

LONGMEADOW
PRESS

A RUNNING HEADS BOOK

Published by Longmeadow Press, 201 High Ridge Road,
Stamford, Connecticut 06904.

THE BIRDWATCHER'S BOOK OF LISTS: Eastern Region
was conceived and produced by
Running Heads Incorporated
55 West 21 Street
New York, NY 10010

Editor: Rose K. Phillips
Art Director/Designer: Gael Towey
Original Paintings: Juan Luis G. Vela
Map Art: Michele Lerner

ISBN 0-681-41477-4

Typeset by David E. Seham Associates Inc., Typographers, Metuchen, N.J.
Color separations by Hong Kong Scanner Craft Company Ltd.
Printed and bound in Hong Kong by C & C Offset Printing Co., Ltd.
0 9 8 7 6 5 4 3 2 1

Companion volume: *The Birdwatcher's Book of Lists:*
Western Region, by Dr. Lester L. Short

The author thanks Jennifer F.M. Horne,
Mary Forsell, and Marta Hallett
for their helpful suggestions,
and Jennifer, especially, for her patience.

. . . .

This book is dedicated to all those working to
save birds and their habitats for posterity;
to the extent that we succeed,
those following will lead a richer life.

Contents

Introduction

PART
1

The Birding Lists

P A R T

2

The Maps

. . . .

APPENDIX SOURCES

This book of lists has been designed so that every birder can better organize and enjoy his or her birdwatching activities. The lists have been created to correspond to natural categories, in an effort to assist the birder in making correct identifications, and keeping a permanent record of these, and to educate the birder to other facets of ornithology. The lists in and of themselves, and the categories they represent, tell much about birds: their seasonality, plumage variations, and habitats. In fact, each list here has been organized so that it brings to the birder an understanding of natural groupings of birds, based variously on a common habitat; a particular group of birds that act in a particular way; a single family, order, or genus of birds; the time of day, month, or year, when a group of birds engages in a particular activity; or the changing plumages of birds, based on the season of the year.

Rather than overwhelm the reader with illustrations that attempt to identify every species included here, we have chosen instead to portray only the more common, widespread, and conspicuous birds of the region covered; that is, the area of North America north of Mexico and east of the 100th meridian. We realize that any experienced birder would have his own selection of such species; this being the author's own. This book is *not* a field guide. In fact, it is an ancillary tool, one that should be used alongside any of the fine field guides available to the birder today.

The twenty-three lists offered here present common, regularly occurring species, and generally exclude unusual or uncommon birds. In dealing with less common species, the principle for the birder to follow is to consider a bird to represent the expected, common species *unless* it can be proved by its features that it is not such. The unexpected *can* happen; but birding, like any other science, generally works within the law of averages, so it should be presumed that the species sighted is the most common one.

This book has been written with the assumption that the

birder will be viewing for the lists from one location. However, our range delineation—that is, north of Mexico east of the 100th meridian in North America—may change some species from "expected" to "unexpected." To help the birder cope with sightings with as much precision as possible, the symbols *N* for north, *S* for south, *E* for east, and *W* for west have been used. These symbols, in parentheses following the English name of the bird on the list, show restriction in occurrence of a species to the part of the region so specified.

The twenty-three lists have been compiled in an order that moves from the commoner, most conspicuous, species, to the most difficult, or those that would necessitate travel from a home environment for completion. This should help the birder to familiarize himself or herself with the techniques of birding, feel the accomplishment of compiling the lists, and move on, with ease, to the more ambitious, difficult lists.

Each of the lists here that have no designated time limitation—that is, in hours or season, for sightings—are presumed to be compiled in a single sighting period, for which the reader will set his or her own time frame. The larger lists relating to habitat are generally exclusive. In other words, a woodland species that enters overgrown pastures will be listed here as a "woodland" rather than a "field" bird. Some birds of open areas that enter open woodlands will be found on the "field" bird list. Those lists that deal with migrant species, as well as the *24-Hour Spring Field Birdwatch* list, involve selecting the most opportune time, or season, for the sighting. In the northeast, for example, mid-May and mid-September provide the seasons with the greatest range of available species. Farther south, in the southeast, the sightings must be accomplished earlier, in April, or even March, for example, to fall into the period considered as the "Spring" season for birds. In terms of time of day for compilation, the *24-Hour Spring Field Birdwatch* list should begin in the dark, in order to be able to spot the widest range of nightbirds. Some birders begin a twenty-four hour watch at 2:00 or 3:00 AM, for example.

The list of *Female Waterfowl* includes fairly common

species that have a distinctive female plumage. The *Immature Birds* species are also those with plumages that are distinct and carried by the birds for a long period: This may be a period of months in smaller birds; or years in some of the larger species. Note that most birds have two non-adult plumages, immature and juvenile, and some even have a downy young plumage. The downy plumage, however, is usually held for a short period, often only when the young are with their parents, so their identities can be discerned by their parents. Also ommitted from the listing of immature birds are those young birds that essentially resemble the adult female so closely that they cannot be readily distinguished from her. It is interesting to note that most immature-plumaged birds show a greater resemblance to the adult female than the adult male, no matter which gender the offspring. The restricted lists, such as *Birds of Prey,* are based on frequently seen species that, in the cases of restriction, are only found in the specified area, or habitat.

Flight identification presents completely different problems for the birder than does the identification of perched species, so included here is a list for completion of those birds that are commonly seen in flight. In the list for *Canadian Border and Mountain Birds,* the symbols *Su* for summer, or breeding, and *Wi* for winter, or nonbreeding, plumages are used.

The *Vagrant Species* list has been designed as a personal tally, for which species are "vagrant" depends on the birder's location for sighting. Irregular events, such as hurricanes, which occur in diverse places, depending on their paths, can bring birds in from afar, but these events vary tremendously in terms of the birds that will be accidentally carried along and, fortunately, major hurricanes are not annual events.

Arctic birds, as defined here, are those species from the high Arctic that do not breed in southern Canada. These birds should be sought in winter, and are generally more likely to be observed in the north than in the south. Night birding should take place during the breeding season, in order to be able to sight the greatest number of species, in that these birds are more plentiful at this time of year. The breeding season for these birds generally means June in the north, but may occur as early as April in the deep south.

The *North American Travel* and *World Travel* lists have been designed to be constructed entirely by the reader. The source for the species in these lists should be the birder's field guide. Rather than catalogue some 9,000 species worldwide or the approximately 840 in North America alone, it is more expedient to allow the reader to compile a personal list.

In addition to the twenty-three lists, a section containing range maps has been included in the book, so that the reader can more precisely verify, by locale, whether a bird has been accurately sighted. Range information—incorporating habitat resident, and winter patterns—can be one of the key factors in making a positive identification. Only rarely will a bird stray from its known habitat and flight pattern. The range maps here are meant to present a diverse array of the different patterns of distribution of birds, including residents, migrants that winter in a part of their breeding range, migrants that move over long distances, and wintering species.

In addition to the lists, illustrations, and range map information, also included is an "Appendix" that provides references, lists of Audubon Societies and addresses, and popular bird-watching periodicals.

English and scientific names used in the listings conform to the 1983 *American Ornithologists' Union Check-list of North American Birds,* Sixth Edition.

As mentioned previously, a good field guide is a necessity for every birdwatcher, and one must be used in conjunction with this book. Some excellent guides are available, including those that pertain to states, or even particular localities. A listing of these can be found in the bibliography in the *Appendix.*

In trying to identify a species, note, and jot down, if possible, all the visible characteristics *before* the bird disappears from sight. A micro-cassette recorder is a great help, for one can whisper characteristics without taking one's eyes from the bird. In addition to general color and size, try to determine the color of beak, legs, feet, and undertail feathers. Notice whether the bird has wing bars, an eye-ring, white on its tail; stripes on its body, a patch on its cheek, or a line over its eyes. Check the shape of its bill. Notice the size, habits, and habitats, and voice of the bird. Any one of these can be an important clue to the identity of the species. In many cases, the bird's English or scientific name is descriptive of one of these factors.

It is our hope that this book will assist you in enjoying North America's birds. Birdwatching is a lifelong "occupation," providing many thrills and enhancing the understanding of man's place in nature. Enjoy your birds and help as you can to preserve their habitats, for throughout the world, and especially in the tropics, we stand to lose for all time, great numbers of species that those coming after us will never see and know. As our understanding of birds grows on a popular level, the greater will be our ability to preserve all the species for viewing by following generations.

LESTER L. SHORT

PART I

The
Birding
Lists

Birdfeeder Birds

PLACE

. . . .

SPECIES SIGHTED

. . . .

NUMBER

SPECIES SIGHTED

♂	♀	JUV.	IMM.	D O V E S
___	___	___	___	Mourning Dove, *Zenaida macroura*
___	___	___	___	Common Ground-Dove(S), *Columbina passerina*

H U M M I N G B I R D S

___	___	___	___	Ruby-throated Hummingbird, *Archilochus colubris*

W O O D P E C K E R S

___	___	___	___	Red-headed Woodpecker, *Melanerpes erythrocephalus*
___	___	___	___	Red-bellied Woodpecker, *Melanerpes carolinus*
___	___	___	___	Downy Woodpecker, *Picoides pubescens*
___	___	___	___	Hairy Woodpecker, *Picoides villosus*
___	___	___	___	Northern Flicker, *Colaptes auratus*

JAYS AND CROWS

	♂	♀	JUV.	IMM.
Blue Jay, *Cyanocitta cristata*	___	___	___	___
Scrub Jay(S), *Aphelocoma coerulescens*	___	___	___	___
American Crow, *Corvus brachyrhynchos*	___	___	___	___

CHICKADEES AND TITMICE

Black-capped Chickadee, *Parus atricapillus*	___	___	___	___
Carolina Chickadee(S), *Parus carolinensis*	___	___	___	___
Boreal Chickadee(N), *Parus hudsonicus*	___	___	___	___
Tufted Titmouse, *Parus bicolor*	___	___	___	___

♂	♀	JUV.	IMM.	NUTHATCHES AND WRENS
—	—	—	—	White-breasted Nuthatch, *Sitta carolinensis*
—	—	—	—	House Wren, *Troglodytes aedon*

THRUSHES AND MOCKINGBIRDS

—	—	—	—	Eastern Bluebird, *Sialia sialis*
—	—	—	—	American Robin, *Turdus migratorius*
—	—	—	—	Northern Mockingbird, *Mimus polyglottos*

STARLINGS

—	—	—	—	European Starling, *Sturnus vulgaris*

CARDINALS GROSBEAKS, AND BUNTINGS

—	—	—	—	Northern Cardinal, *Cardinalis cardinalis*
—	—	—	—	Rose-breasted Grosbeak, *Pheucticus ludovicianus*
—	—	—	—	Painted Bunting(S), *Passerina ciris*

TOWHEES, SPARROWS, AND JUNCOS

—	—	—	—	Rufous-sided Towhee, *Pipilo erythrophthalmus*
—	—	—	—	American Tree Sparrow(N), *Spizella arborea*
—	—	—	—	Chipping Sparrow, *Spizella passerina*
—	—	—	—	Field Sparrow, *Spizella pusilla*

	♂	♀	JUV.	IMM.

Fox Sparrow, *Passerella iliaca*

Song Sparrow, *Melospiza melodia*

White-throated Sparrow, *Zonotrichia albicollis*

White-crowned Sparrow, *Zonotrichia leucophrys*

Dark-eyed Junco, *Junco hyemalis*

BLACKBIRDS AND ALLIES

Red-winged Blackbird, *Agelaius phoeniceus*

Boat-tailed Grackle, *Quiscalus major*

Common Grackle, *Quiscalus quiscula*

Brown-headed Cowbird, *Molothrus ater*

FINCHES AND ALLIES

Purple Finch, *Carpodacus purpureus*

House Finch, *Carpodacus mexicanus*

Common Redpoll (N), *Carduelis flammea*

Pine Siskin, *Carduelis pinus*

American Goldfinch, *Carduelis tristis*

Evening Grosbeak (N), *Coccothraustes verpertinus*

House Sparrow, *Passer domesticus*

Month-by-Month Backyard Birdwatch

FOR YEAR

. . . .

AT

. . . .

P L A C E

J A N U A R Y

_____ _____ _____

_____ _____ _____

_____ _____ _____

F E B R U A R Y

_____ _____ _____

_____ _____ _____

_____ _____ _____

M A R C H

_____ _____ _____

_____ _____ _____

_____ _____ _____

A P R I L

_____ _____ _____

_____ _____ _____

_____ _____ _____

M A Y

_____ _____ _____

_____ _____ _____

_____ _____ _____

J U N E

_____ _____ _____

_____ _____ _____

_____ _____ _____

JULY

_____ _____ _____

_____ _____ _____

_____ _____ _____

_____ _____ _____

AUGUST

_____ _____ _____

_____ _____ _____

_____ _____ _____

_____ _____ _____

SEPTEMBER

_____ _____ _____

_____ _____ _____

_____ _____ _____

_____ _____ _____

O C T O B E R

. . . .

_____ _____ _____

_____ _____ _____

_____ _____ _____

_____ _____ _____

N O V E M B E R

_____ _____ _____

_____ _____ _____

_____ _____ _____

_____ _____ _____

D E C E M B E R

_____ _____ _____

_____ _____ _____

_____ _____ _____

_____ _____ _____

Nesting Yard Species

**AND
ENDING ON**

. . . .
D A T E

AT

. . . .
P L A C E

SPECIES SIGHTED
(Fill in ♂, ♀, Juv., or Imm.)

DOVES

_____ Mourning Dove, *Zenaida macroura*

_____ Common Ground-Dove, *Columbina passerina*

WOODPECKERS

_____ Red-headed Woodpecker, *Melanerpes erythrocephalus*

_____ Red-bellied Woodpecker, *Melanerpes carolinus*

_____ Downy Woodpecker, *Picoides pubescens*

_____ Red-cockaded Woodpecker, *Picoides borealis*

_____ Northern Flicker, *Colaptes auratus*

SWALLOWS, JAYS, AND CROWS

_____ Purple Martin, *Progne subis*

_____ Tree Swallow, *Tachycineta bicolor*

_____ Barn Swallow, *Hirundo rustica*

_____ Blue Jay, *Cyanocitta cristata*

_____ American Crow, *Corvus brachyrhynchos*

CHICKADEES, TITMICE, NUTHATCHES, WRENS, AND THRUSHES

_____ Black-capped Chickadee, *Parus atricapillus*

Carolina Chickadee(S), *Parus carolinensis* ⎯⎯⎯

Tufted Titmouse, *Parus bicolor* ⎯⎯⎯

Red-breasted Nuthatch, *Sitta canadensis* ⎯⎯⎯

Carolina Wren, *Thryothorus ludovicianus* ⎯⎯⎯

House Wren, *Troglodytes aedon* ⎯⎯⎯

Eastern Bluebird, *Sialia sialis* ⎯⎯⎯

Wood Thrush, *Hylocichla mustelina* ⎯⎯⎯

American Robin, *Turdus migratorius* ⎯⎯⎯

MOCKINGBIRDS AND ALLIES

Gray Catbird, *Dumetella carolinensis* ⎯⎯⎯

Northern Mockingbird, *Mimus polyglottos* ⎯⎯⎯

Brown Thrasher, *Toxostoma rufum* ⎯⎯⎯

European Starling, *Sturnus vulgarls* ⎯⎯⎯

CARDINALS AND ALLIES

Northern Cardinal, *Cardinalis cardinalis* ⎯⎯⎯

Rose-breasted Grosbeak, *Pheucticus ludovicianus* ⎯⎯⎯

Painted Bunting, *Passerina ciris* ⎯⎯⎯

Rufous-sided Towhee, *Pipilo erythrophthalmus* ⎯⎯⎯

Cassin's Sparrow, *Aimophila cassinii* ⎯⎯⎯

Chipping Sparrow, *Spizella passerina* ⎯⎯⎯

Song Sparrow, *Melospiza melodia* ⎯⎯⎯

BLACKBIRDS, ORIOLES, FINCHES, AND ALLIES

Common Grackle, *Quiscalus quiscula* ⎯⎯⎯

Brown-headed Cowbird, *Molothrus ater* ⎯⎯⎯

Orchard Oriole(S), *Icterus spurius* ⎯⎯⎯

Northern Oriole, *Icterus galbula* ⎯⎯⎯

House Finch, *Carpodacus mexicanus* ⎯⎯⎯

House Sparrow, *Passer domesticus* ⎯⎯⎯

Coastal Waterbirds

DATE

. . . .

PLACE

. . . .

**SPECIES
SIGHTED**

. . . .

NUMBER

SPECIES SIGHTED

♂ ♀ JUV. IMM. LOONS AND
GREBES

—— —— —— —— Red-throated Loon, *Gavia
stellata*

—— —— —— —— Common Loon, *Gavia immer*

—— —— —— —— Horned Grebe, *Podiceps
auritus*

—— —— —— —— Red-necked Grebe, *Podiceps
grisegena*

PELICANS AND
CORMORANTS

—— —— —— —— Brown Pelican(S), *Pelecanus
occidentalis*

—— —— —— —— Great Cormorant(N),
Phalacrocorax carbo

—— —— —— —— Double-crested Cormorant,
Phalacrocorax auritus

HERONS, IBISES, AND SPOONBILLS

	♂	♀	JUV.	IMM.
Great Blue Heron, *Ardea herodias*				
Great Egret, *Casmerodius albus*				
Snowy Egret, *Egretta thula*				
Tricolored Heron(S), *Egretta tricolor*				
Reddish Egret(S), *Egretta rufescens*				
Black-crowned Night-Heron, *Nycticorax nycticorax*				
Yellow-crowned Night-Heron, *Nycticorax violaceus*				
White Ibis(S), *Eudocimus albus*				
Glossy Ibis, *Plegadis falcinellus*				
Roseate Spoonbill(S), *Ajaia ajaja*				

♂	♀	JUV.	IMM.	SWANS, GEESE, AND DUCKS
___	___	___	___	Mute Swan(N), *Cygnus olor*
___	___	___	___	Brant, *Branta bernicla*
___	___	___	___	Canada Goose(N), *Branta canadensis*
___	___	___	___	American Black Duck(N), *Anas rubripes*
___	___	___	___	Northern Shoveler, *Anas clypeata*
___	___	___	___	Canvasback, *Aythya valisineria*
___	___	___	___	Redhead, *Aythya americana*
___	___	___	___	Greater Scaup, *Aythya marila*
___	___	___	___	Lesser Scaup, *Aythya affinis*
___	___	___	___	Common Eider, *Somateria mollissima*
___	___	___	___	King Eider(N), *Somateria spectabilis*
___	___	___	___	Harlequin Duck(N), *Histrionicus histrionicus*
___	___	___	___	Oldsquaw(N), *Clangula hyemalis*
___	___	___	___	Black Scoter(N), *Melanitta nigra*
___	___	___	___	Surf Scoter, *Melanitta perspicillata*
___	___	___	___	White-winged Scoter, *Melanitta fusca*
___	___	___	___	Common Goldeneye, *Bucephala clangula*
___	___	___	___	Barrow's Goldeneye(N), *Bucephala islandica*
___	___	___	___	Bufflehead, *Bucephala albeola*
___	___	___	___	Common Merganser, *Mergus merganser*
___	___	___	___	Red-breasted Merganser, *Mergus serrator*
___	___	___	___	Ruddy Duck, *Oxyura jamaicensis*

EAGLES AND HAWKS	♂	♀	JUV.	IMM.
Bald Eagle, *Haliaeetus leucocephalus*	—	—	—	—
Northern Harrier, *Circus cyaneus*	—	—	—	—

RAILS, GALLINULES, COOTS, AND LIMPKINS

	♂	♀	JUV.	IMM.
Black Rail, *Laterallus jamaicensis*	—	—	—	—
Clapper Rail, *Rallus longirostris*	—	—	—	—
Virginia Rail, *Rallus limicola*	—	—	—	—
Sora, *Porzana carolina*	—	—	—	—
Common Moorhen, *Gallinula chloropus*	—	—	—	—
American Coot, *Fulica americana*	—	—	—	—
Limpkin(S), *Aramus guarauna*	—	—	—	

PLOVERS, OYSTERCATCHERS, SANDPIPERS, AND ALLIES

	♂	♀	JUV.	IMM.
Black-bellied Plover, *Pluvialis squatarola*	—	—	—	—
Wilson's Plover, *Charadrius wilsonia*	—	—	—	—
Piping Plover, *Charadrius melodus*	—	—	—	—
Killdeer, *Charadrius vociferus*	—	—	—	—
American Oystercatcher, *Haematopus palliatus*	—	—	—	—

♂	♀	JUV.	IMM.	
——	——	——	——	Greater Yellowlegs, *Tringa melanoleuca*
——	——	——	——	Lesser Yellowlegs, *Tringa flavipes*
——	——	——	——	Willet, *Catoptrophorus semipalmatus*
——	——	——	——	Spotted Sandpiper, *Actitis macularia*
——	——	——	——	Ruddy Turnstone, *Arenaria interpres*
——	——	——	——	Red Knot, *Calidris canutus*
——	——	——	——	Sanderling, *Calidris alba*
——	——	——	——	Semipalmated Sandpiper, *Calidris pusilla*
——	——	——	——	Western Sandpiper, *Calidris mauri*
——	——	——	——	Least Sandpiper, *Calidris minutilla*
——	——	——	——	Purple Sandpiper, *Calidris maritima*
——	——	——	——	Dunlin, *Calidris alpina*
——	——	——	——	Curlew Sandpiper, *Calidris ferruginea*
——	——	——	——	Short-billed Dowitcher, *Limnodromus griseus*
——	——	——	——	Common Snipe, *Gallinago gallinago*

GULLS, TERNS, AND SKIMMERS

♂	♀	JUV.	IMM.	
——	——	——	——	Laughing Gull(S), *Larus atricilla*
——	——	——	——	Ring-billed Gull, *Larus delawarensis*
——	——	——	——	Herring Gull, *Larus argentatus*
——	——	——	——	Ivory Gull, *Pagophila eburnea*
——	——	——	——	Caspian Tern, *Sterna caspia*
——	——	——	——	Common Tern, *Sterna hirundo*

	♂	♀	JUV.	IMM.
Least Tern, *Sterna antillarum*	—	—	—	—
Black Tern, *Chlidonias niger*	—	—	—	—
Black Skimmer, *Rynchops niger*	—	—	—	—

OWLS AND KINGFISHERS

	♂	♀	JUV.	IMM.
Short-eared Owl, *Asio flammeus*	—	—	—	—
Belted Kingfisher, *Ceryle alcyon*	—	—	—	—

SWALLOWS AND CROWS

	♂	♀	JUV.	IMM.
Barn Swallow, *Hirundo rustica*	—	—	—	—
Fish Crow, *Corvus ossifragus*	—	—	—	—

WRENS

	♂	♀	JUV.	IMM.
Marsh Wren, *Cistothorus palustris*	—	—	—	—

SPARROWS

	♂	♀	JUV.	IMM.
Savannah Sparrow, *Passerculus sandwichensis*	—	—	—	—
Sharp-tailed Sparrow, *Ammodramus caudacutus*	—	—	—	—
Seaside Sparrow, *Ammodramus maritimus*	—	—	—	—

BLACKBIRDS

	♂	♀	JUV.	IMM.
Red-winged Blackbird (S), *Agelaius phoeniceus*	—	—	—	—
Boat-tailed Grackle, *Quiscalus major*	—	—	—	—
Common Grackle, *Quiscalus quiscula*	—	—	—	—

Inland Waterbirds

DATE

. . . .

PLACE

. . . .

**SPECIES
SIGHTED**

. . . .

NUMBER

SPECIES SIGHTED

♂   ♀   JUV.   IMM.   **LOONS AND
GREBES**

—— —— —— —— Common Loon, *Gavia immer*

—— —— —— —— Pied-billed Grebe, *Podilymbus
podiceps*

—— —— —— —— Horned Grebe, *Podiceps
auritus*

—— —— —— —— Western Grebe(W),
Aechmophorus occidentalis

**CORMORANTS
AND DARTERS**

—— —— —— —— Double-crested Cormorant(N),
Phalacrocorax auritus

—— —— —— —— Anhinga(S), *Anhinga anhinga*

BITTERNS, HERONS, IBISES, AND STORKS

	♂	♀	JUV.	IMM.
American Bittern, *Botaurus lentiginosus*	—	—	—	—
Least Bittern, *Ixobrychus exilis*	—	—	—	—
Great Blue Heron, *Ardea herodias*	—	—	—	—
Great Egret, *Casmerodius albus*	—	—	—	—
Snowy Egret, *Egretta thula*	—	—	—	—
Little Blue Heron, *Egretta caerulea*	—	—	—	—
Cattle Egret, *Bubulcus ibis*	—	—	—	—
Green-backed Heron, *Butorides striatus*	—	—	—	—

♂	♀	JUV.	IMM.	
___	___	___	___	Black-crowned Night-Heron, *Nycticorax nycticorax*
___	___	___	___	Yellow-crowned Night-Heron, *Nycticorax violaceus*
___	___	___	___	Glossy Ibis, *Plegadis falcinellus*
___	___	___	___	Wood Stork(S), *Mycteria americana*

SWANS, GEESE, AND DUCKS

___	___	___	___	Tundra Swan, *Cygnus columbianus*
___	___	___	___	Mute Swan, *Cygnus olor*
___	___	___	___	Snow Goose, *Chen caerulescens*
___	___	___	___	Canada Goose(N), *Branta canadensis*
___	___	___	___	Wood Duck, *Aix sponsa*
___	___	___	___	Green-winged Teal, *Anas crecca*
___	___	___	___	American Black Duck(N), *Anas rubripes*
___	___	___	___	Mallard, *Anas platyrhynchos*
___	___	___	___	Northern Pintail, *Anas acuta*
___	___	___	___	Blue-winged Teal, *Anas discors*
___	___	___	___	Northern Shoveler, *Anas clypeata*
___	___	___	___	Gadwall, *Anas strepera*
___	___	___	___	American Wigeon, *Anas americana*
___	___	___	___	Canvasback, *Aythya valisineria*
___	___	___	___	Redhead, *Aythya americana*
___	___	___	___	Ring-necked Duck, *Aythya collaris*
___	___	___	___	Greater Scaup, *Aythya marila*
___	___	___	___	Lesser Scaup, *Aythya affinis*

	♂	♀	JUV.	IMM.

White-winged Scoter, *Melanitta fusca* — — — —

Common Goldeneye, *Bucephala clangula* — — — —

Bufflehead(N), *Bucephala albeola* — — — —

Hooded Merganser, *Lophodytes cucullatus* — — — —

Common Merganser, *Mergus merganser* — — — —

Ruddy Duck, *Oxyura jamaicensis* — — — —

KITES, EAGLES, HAWKS, AND ALLIES

Osprey, *Pandion haliaetus* — — — —

Bald Eagle, *Haliaeetus leucocephalus* — — — —

Northern Harrier, *Circus cyaneus* — — — —

RAILS, COOTS, LIMPKINS, AND CRANES

Yellow Rail, *Coturnicops noveboracensis* — — — —

King Rail, *Rallus elegans* — — — —

Virginia Rail, *Rallus limicola* — — — —

Sora, *Porzana carolina* — — — —

Common Moorhen, *Gallinula chloropus* — — — —

American Coot, *Fulica americana* — — — —

Limpkin(S), *Aramus guarauna* — — — —

♂	♀	JUV.	IMM.	PLOVERS, SANDPIPERS, AND ALLIES
___	___	___	___	Sandhill Crane, *Grus canadensis*
___	___	___	___	Black-bellied Plover, *Pluvialis squatarola*
___	___	___	___	Lesser Golden-Plover, *Pluvialis apricaria*
___	___	___	___	Killdeer, *Charadrius vociferus*
___	___	___	___	Greater Yellowlegs, *Tringa melanoleuca*
___	___	___	___	Lesser Yellowlegs, *Tringa flavipes*
___	___	___	___	Spotted Sandpiper, *Actitis macularia*
___	___	___	___	Whimbrel, *Numenius phaeopus*
___	___	___	___	Semipalmated Sandpiper, *Calidris pusilla*
___	___	___	___	Western Sandpiper, *Calidris mauri*
___	___	___	___	Dunlin, *Calidris alpina*
___	___	___	___	Short-billed Dowitcher, *Limnodromus griseus*

GULLS AND TERNS

♂	♀	JUV.	IMM.	
___	___	___	___	Ring-billed Gull, *Larus delawarensis*
___	___	___	___	Herring Gull, *Larus argentatus*
___	___	___	___	Common Tern, *Sterna hirundo*
___	___	___	___	Least Tern, *Sterna antillarum*
___	___	___	___	Black Tern, *Chlidonias niger*

KINGFISHERS   ♂   ♀   JUV.   IMM.

Belted Kingfisher, *Ceryle alcyon* ___ ___ ___ ___

FLYCATCHERS AND SWALLOWS

Alder Flycatcher, *Empidonax alnorum* ___ ___ ___ ___

Tree Swallow, *Tachycineta bicolor* ___ ___ ___ ___

Bank Swallow, *Riparia riparia* ___ ___ ___ ___

Rough-Winged Swallow, *Stelgidopteryx ruficollis* ___ ___ ___ ___

Barn Swallow, *Hirundo rustica* ___ ___ ___ ___

PIPITS

Water Pipit, *Anthus spinoletta* ___ ___ ___ ___

WARBLERS

Northern Waterthrush, *Seiurus noveboracensis* ___ ___ ___ ___

Common Yellowthroat, *Geothlypis trichas* ___ ___ ___ ___

SPARROWS

Song Sparrow, *Melospiza melodia* ___ ___ ___ ___

Lincoln's Sparrow, *Melospiza lincolnii* ___ ___ ___ ___

Swamp Sparrow, *Melospiza georgiana* ___ ___ ___ ___

BLACKBIRDS

Red-winged Blackbird, *Agelaius phoeniceus* ___ ___ ___ ___

Rusty Blackbird, *Euphagus carolinus* ___ ___ ___ ___

Female Waterfowl

FEMALE DUCKS AND ALLIES

Family Anatidae *(by Genus)*

DATE

. . . .

PLACE

. . . .

SPECIES SIGHTED

. . . .

NUMBER

GENUS *Aix*
_____ Wood Duck, *Aix sponsa*

GENUS *Anas*
_____ Green-winged Teal, *Anas crecca*
_____ Mallard, *Anas platyrhynchos*
_____ Northern Pintail, *Anas acuta*
_____ Blue-winged Teal, *Anas discors*
_____ Northern Shoveler, *Anas clypeata*
_____ Gadwall, *Anas strepera*
_____ American Wigeon, *Anas americana*

GENUS *Aythya*
_____ Canvasback, *Aythya valisineria*
_____ Redhead, *Aythya americana*

Ring-necked Duck, *Aythya collaris* _____

Greater Scaup, *Aythya marila* _____

Lesser Scaup, *Aythya affinis* _____

GENUS *Somateria*

Common Eider, *Somateria mollissima* _____

GENUS *Clangula*

Oldsquaw(N), *Clangula hyemalis* _____

GENUS *Melanitta*

Black Scoter, *Melanitta nigra* _____

Surf Scoter, *Melanitta perspicillata* _____

White-winged Scoter, *Melanitta fusca* _____

GENUS *Bucephala*

Common Goldeneye, *Bucephala clangula* _____

Bufflehead(N), *Bucephala albeola* _____

GENUS *Lophodytes*

Hooded Merganser, *Lophodytes cucullatus* _____

GENUS *Mergus*

Common Merganser, *Mergus merganser* _____

Red-breasted Merganser, *Mergus serrator* _____

GENUS *Oxyura*

Ruddy Duck, *Oxyura jamaicensis* _____

Immature Birds

♂ ♀ GANNETS, PELICANS, HERONS, AND SWANS

___ ___ Northern Gannet(N), *Sula bassanus*

___ ___ Brown Pelican(S), *Pelecanus occidentalis*

___ ___ Black-crowned Night-Heron, *Nycticorax nycticorax*

___ ___ Yellow-crowned Night-Heron(S), *Nycticorax violaceus*

___ ___ White Ibis(S), *Eudocimus albus*

___ ___ Mute Swan(N), *Cygnus olor*

DATE

. . . .

PLACE

. . . .

SPECIES SIGHTED

. . . .

NUMBER

BIRDS OF PREY

___ ___ Bald Eagle, *Haliaeetus leucocephalus*

___ ___ Sharp-shinned Hawk, *Accipiter striatus*

___ ___ Cooper's Hawk, *Accipiter cooperii*

___ ___ Red-tailed Hawk, *Buteo jamaicensis*

___ ___ Rough-legged Hawk(N), *Buteo lagopus*

___ ___ Merlin, *Falco columbarius*

___ ___ Peregrine Falcon, *Falco peregrinus*

GALLINULES

___ ___ Common Moorhen, *Gallinula chloropus*

GULLS

___ ___ Laughing Gull, *Larus atricilla*

___ ___ Bonaparte's Gull, *Larus philadelphia*

___ ___ Ring-billed Gull, *Larus delawarensis*

DOVES

___ ___ Mourning Dove, *Zenaida macroura*

OWLS AND WOODPECKERS

	♂	♀
Northern Saw-whet Owl(N), *Aegolius acadicus*	—	—
Red-headed Woodpecker, *Melanerpes erythrocephalus*	—	—
Yellow-bellied Sapsucker, *Sphyrapicus varius*	—	—

SWALLOWS, THRUSHES, AND STARLINGS

Tree Swallow, *Tachycineta bicolor*	—	—
American Robin, *Turdus migratorius*	—	—
European Starling, *Sturnus vulgaris*	—	—

WARBLERS

Yellow-rumped Warbler, *Dendroica coronata*	—	—
American Redstart, *Setophaga ruticilla*	—	—

GROSBEAKS AND SPARROWS

Blue Grosbeak, *Guiraca caerulea*	—	—
Indigo Bunting, *Passerina cyanea*	—	—
Chipping Sparrow, *Spizella passerina*	—	—

BLACKBIRDS AND ORIOLES

Red-winged Blackbird, *Agelaius phoeniceus*	—	—
Orchard Oriole, *Icterus spurius*	—	—
Northern Oriole, *Icterus galbula*	—	—

COMMENTS AND SIGHTING NOTES

. . . .

Birds of Prey

SIGHTINGS OF VULTURES, EAGLES, AND HAWKS

Families Cathartidae *and* Accipitridae

♂ ♀ JUV. IMM. VULTURES

—— —— —— —— Black Vulture(S), *Coragyps atratus*

—— —— —— —— Turkey Vulture, *Cathartes aura*

DATE

. . . .

PLACE

. . . .

SPECIES SIGHTED

. . . .

NUMBER

EAGLES AND HAWKS

—— —— —— —— Osprey, *Pandion haliaetus*

—— —— —— —— Bald Eagle, *Haliaeetus leucocephalus*

—— —— —— —— Northern Harrier, *Circus cyaneus*

—— —— —— —— Sharp-shinned Hawk, *Accipiter striatus*

—— —— —— —— Cooper's Hawk, *Accipiter cooperii*

—— —— —— —— Red-shouldered Hawk, *Buteo lineatus*

—— —— —— —— Broad-winged Hawk, *Buteo platypterus*

—— —— —— —— Swainson's Hawk(W), *Buteo swainsoni*

—— —— —— —— Red-tailed Hawk, *Buteo jamaicensis*

	♂	♀	JUV.	IMM.
Ferruginous Hawk, *Buteo regalis*	___	___	___	___
Rough-legged Hawk, *Buteo lagopus*	___	___	___	___
Golden Eagle, *Aquila chrysaetos*	___	___	___	___

FALCONS

	♂	♀	JUV.	IMM.
American Kestrel, *Falco sparverius*	___	___	___	___
Merlin, *Falco columbarius*	___	___	___	___
Peregrine Falcon, *Falco peregrinus*	___	___	___	___
Gyrfalcon, *Falco rusticolus*	___	___	___	___

COMMENTS AND SIGHTING NOTES

. . . .

Woodland Birds in Spring Plumages

BEGINNING ON

. . . .

D A T E

AND ENDING ON

. . . .

D A T E

AT

. . . .

P L A C E

SPECIES SIGHTED

(Fill in ♂, ♀, Juv., or Imm.)

HERONS, IBISES, AND SPOONBILLS

_____ American Bittern, *Botaurus lentiginosus*

_____ Least Bittern, *Ixobrychus exilis*

_____ Great Blue Heron, *Ardea herodias*

_____ Great Egret, *Casmerodius albus*

_____ Snowy Egret, *Egretta thula*

_____ Little Blue Heron, *Egretta caerulea*

_____ Tricolored Heron, *Egretta tricolor*

_____ Reddish Egret, *Egretta rufescens*

_____ Cattle Egret, *Bubulcus ibis*

_____ Green-backed Heron, *Butorides striatus*

_____ Black-crowned Night-Heron, *Nycticorax nycticorax*

_____ Yellow-crowned Night-Heron, *Nycticorax violaceus*

_____ White Ibis, *Eudocimus albus*

_____ Glossy Ibis, *Plegadis falcinellus*

_____ White-faced Ibis, *Plegadis chihi*

_____ Roseate Spoonbill, *Ajaia ajaja*

DUCKS

_____ Wood Duck, *Aix sponsa*

_____ American Black Duck(N), *Anas rubripes*

_____ Common Goldeneye(N), *Bucephala clangula*

_____ Hooded Merganser, *Lophodytes cucullatus*

VULTURES

_____ Black Vulture(S), *Coragyps atratus*

_____ Turkey Vulture, *Cathartes aura*

KITES, HAWKS, AND FALCONS

American Swallow-tailed Kite, _____
Elanoides forficatus

Sharp-shinned Hawk, _____
Accipiter striatus

Cooper's Hawk, _____
Accipiter cooperii

Northern Goshawk(N), _____
Accipiter gentilis

Red-shouldered Hawk, _____
Buteo lineatus

Broad-winged Hawk, _____
Buteo platypterus

Red-tailed Hawk, _____
Buteo jamaicensis

Merlin(N), _____
Falco columbarius

GROUSE AND TURKEYS

Spruce Grouse(N), _____
Dendragapus canadensis

Ruffed Grouse(N), *Bonasa umbellus* _____

Wild Turkey(S), *Meleagris gallopavo* _____

WOODCOCK

American Woodcock, *Scolopax minor* _____

DOVES AND CUCKOOS

Mourning Dove, *Zenaida macroura* _____

Black-billed Cuckoo, _____
Coccyzus erythropthalmus

Yellow-billed Cuckoo, _____
Coccyzus americanus

OWLS

_____ Eastern Screech-Owl, *Otus asio*

_____ Great Horned Owl, *Bubo virginianus*

_____ Barred Owl, *Strix varia*

_____ Long-eared Owl(N), *Asio otus*

_____ Northern Saw-whet Owl(N), *Aegolius acadicus*

GOATSUCKERS

_____ Chuck-will's-widow(S), *Caprimulgus carolinensis*

_____ Whip-poor-will, *Caprimulgus vociferus*

SWIFTS AND HUMMINGBIRDS

_____ Chimney Swift, *Chaetura pelagica*

_____ Ruby-throated Hummingbird, *Archilochus colubris*

KINGFISHERS, WOODPECKERS, AND ALLIES

_____ Belted Kingfisher, *Ceryle alcyon*

_____ Red-headed Woodpecker, *Melanerpes erythrocephalus*

_____ Red-bellied Woodpecker, *Melanerpes carolinus*

_____ Yellow-bellied Sapsucker, *Sphyrapicus varius*

_____ Downy Woodpecker, *Picoides pubescens*

_____ Hairy Woodpecker, *Picoides villosus*

_____ Red-cockaded Woodpecker(S), *Picoides borealis*

_____ Three-toed Woodpecker(N), *Picoides tridactylus*

_____ Black-backed Woodpecker(N), *Picoides arcticus*

_____ Northern Flicker, *Colaptes auratus*

_____ Pileated Woodpecker, *Dryocopus pileatus*

FLYCATCHERS

Olive-sided Flycatcher, *Mionectes olivaceus* _____

Eastern Wood-Pewee, *Contopus virens* _____

Yellow-bellied Flycatcher(N), *Empidonax flaviventris* _____

Acadian Flycatcher, *Empidonax virescens* _____

Least Flycatcher(N), *Empidonax minimus* _____

Eastern Phoebe, *Sayornis phoebe* _____

Eastern Kingbird, *Tyrannus tyrannus* _____

Gray Kingbird, *Tyrannus dominicensis* _____

SWALLOWS

Tree Swallow(N), *Tachycineta bicolor* _____

Barn Swallow, *Hirundo rustica* _____

JAYS AND CROWS

Gray Jay(N), *Perisoreus canadensis* _____

Blue Jay, *Cyanocitta cristata* _____

Scrub Jay(S), *Aphelocoma coerulescens* _____

American Crow, *Corvus brachyrhynchos* _____

Fish Crow, *Corvus ossifragus* _____

Common Raven(N), *Corvus corax* _____

CHICKADEES

Black-capped Chickadee(N), *Parus atricapillus* _____

Carolina Chickadee(S), *Parus carolinensis* _____

Boreal Chickadee(N), *Parus hudsonicus* _____

NUTHATCHES, CREEPERS, AND WRENS

Red-breasted Nuthatch(N), *Sitta canadensis* _____

Brown-headed Nuthatch, *Sitta pusilla* _____

Brown Creeper, *Certhia americana* _____

Carolina Wren, *Thryothorus ludovicianus* _____

Bewick's Wren, *Thryomanes bewickii* _____

_____ House Wren, *Troglodytes aedon*

_____ Winter Wren(N), *Troglodytes troglodytes*

KINGLETS AND GNATCATCHERS

_____ Golden-crowned Kinglet, *Regulus satrapa*

_____ Ruby-crowned Kinglet, *Regulus calendula*

_____ Blue-gray Gnatcatcher, *Polioptila caerulea*

THRUSHES AND ALLIES

_____ Eastern Bluebird, *Sialia sialis*

_____ Veery(N), *Catharus fuscescens*

_____ Gray-cheeked Thrush(N), *Catharus minimus*

_____ Swainson's Thrush(N), *Catharus ustulatus*

_____ Hermit Thrush(N), *Catharus guttatus*

_____ Wood Thrush, *Hylocichla mustelina*

_____ American Robin, *Turdus migratorius*

MOCKINGBIRDS AND THRASHERS

_____ Gray Catbird, *Dumetella carolinensis*

_____ Northern Mockingbird, *Mimus polyglottos*

_____ Brown Thrasher, *Toxostoma rufum*

WAXWINGS, STARLINGS, AND VIREOS

_____ Cedar Waxwing(N), *Bombycilla cedrorum*

_____ European Starling, *Sturnus vulgaris*

_____ White-eyed Vireo(S), *Vireo griseus*

_____ Bell's Vireo(W), *Vireo bellii*

_____ Solitary Vireo, *Vireo solitarius*

_____ Yellow-throated Vireo, *Vireo flavifrons*

_____ Warbling Vireo, *Vireo gilvus*

_____ Philadelphia Vireo(N), *Vireo philadelphicus*

_____ Red-eyed Vireo, *Vireo olivaceus*

WARBLERS

Blue-winged Warbler, *Vermivora pinus* _____

Golden-winged Warbler (N), *Vermivora chrysoptera* _____

Tennessee Warbler (N), *Vermivora peregrina* _____

Nashville Warbler (N), *Vermivora ruficapilla* _____

Northern Parula, *Parula americana* _____

Yellow Warbler, *Dendroica petechia* _____

Chestnut-sided Warbler (N), *Dendroica pensylvanica* _____

Magnolia Warbler (N), *Dendroica magnolia* _____

Cape May Warbler (N), *Dendroica tigrina* _____

Black-throated Blue Warbler (N), *Dendroica caerulescens* _____

Yellow-rumped Warbler (N), *Dendroica coronata* _____

Black-throated Green Warbler (N), *Dendroica virens* _____

Blackburnian Warbler (N), *Dendroica fusca* _____

Yellow-throated Warbler (S), *Dendroica dominica* _____

Pine Warbler, *Dendroica pinus* _____

Prairie Warbler, *Dendroica discolor* _____

Palm Warbler (N), *Dendroica palmarum* _____

Bay-breasted Warbler (N), *Dendroica castanea* _____

Cerulean Warbler, *Dendroica cerulea* _____

Black-and-white Warbler, *Mniotilta varia* _____

American Redstart, *Setophage ruticilla* _____

Prothonotary Warbler, *Protonotaria citrea* _____

Worm-eating Warbler, *Helmitheros vermivorus* _____

Swainson's Warbler (S), *Limnothlypis swainsonii* _____

Ovenbird, *Seiurus aurocapillus* _____

Northern Waterthrush (N), *Seiurus noveboracensis* _____

_____ Louisiana Waterthrush, *Seiurus motacilla*

_____ Kentucky Warbler, *Oporornis formosus*

_____ Mourning Warbler (N), *Oporornis philadelphia*

_____ Common Yellowthroat, *Geothlypis trichas*

_____ Hooded Warbler, *Wilsonia citrina*

_____ Wilson's Warbler (N), *Wilsonia pusilla*

_____ Canada Warbler (N), *Wilsonia candensis*

TANAGERS, CARDINALS, AND GROSBEAKS

_____ Summer Tanager (S), *Piranga rubra*

_____ Scarlet Tanager, *Piranga olivacea*

_____ Northern Cardinal, *Cardinalis cardinalis*

_____ Rose-breasted Grosbeak, *Pheucticus ludovicianus*

_____ Blue Grosbeak (S), *Guiraca caerulea*

_____ Indigo Bunting, *Passerina cyanea*

_____ Painted Bunting (S), *Passerina ciris*

TOWHEES, SPARROWS, AND ALLIES

_____ Rufous-sided Towhee, *Pipilo erythrophthalmus*

_____ Bachman's Sparrow (S), *Aimophila aestivalis*

_____ Chipping Sparrow, *Spizella passerina*

Clay-colored Sparrow(NW), *Spizella pallida* _____

Lark Sparrow(W), *Chondestes grammacus* _____

Song Sparrow, *Melospiza melodia* _____

Lincoln's Sparrow(N), *Melospiza lincolnii* _____

Swamp Sparrow, *Melospiza georgiana* _____

White-throated Sparrow, *Zonotrichia albicollis* _____

Dark-eyed Junco(N), *Junco hyemalis* _____

BLACKBIRDS AND ORIOLES

Rusty Blackbird(N), *Euphagus carolinus* _____

Common Grackle, *Quiscalus quiscula* _____

Brown-headed Cowbird, *Molothrus ater* _____

Orchard Oriole, *Icterus spurius* _____

Northern Oriole, *Icterus galbula* _____

FINCHES AND ALLIES

Pine Grosbeak(N), *Pinicola enucleator* _____

Purple Finch(N), *Carpodacus purpureus* _____

House Finch, *Carpodacus mexicanus* _____

Red Crossbill(N), *Loxia curvirostra* _____

White-winged Crossbill(N), *Loxia leucoptera* _____

Pine Siskin(N), *Carduelis pinus* _____

Evening Grosbeak(N), *Coccothraustes verpertinus* _____

The Nightbird Search

BEGINNING AT

. . . .
T   I   M   E

AND ENDING AT

. . . .
T   I   M   E

ON

. . . .
D   A   T   E

AT

. . . .
P   L   A   C   E

SPECIES SIGHTED

(Fill in ♂, ♀, Juv., or Imm.)

_____ Common Barn-Owl, *Tyto alba*

_____ Eastern Screech-Owl, *Otus asio*

_____ Great Horned Owl, *Bubo virginianus*

_____ Barred Owl, *Strix varia*

_____ Great Gray Owl, *Strix nebulosa*

_____ Long-eared Owl, *Asio otus*

_____ Short-eared Owl, *Asio flammeus*

_____ Northern Saw-whet Owl, *Aegolius acadicus*

_____ Common Nighthawk, *Chordeiles minor*

_____ Common Poorwill(W), *Phalaenoptilus nuttallii*

_____ Chuck-will's-widow, *Caprimulgus carolinensis*

_____ Whip-poor-will, *Caprimulgus vociferus*

The 24-Hour Spring Field Birdwatch

DATE

. . . .

PLACE

. . . .

SPECIES SIGHTED

. . . .

N U M B E R

SPECIES SIGHTED

♂ ♀ JUV. IMM. VULTURES

—— —— —— —— Turkey Vulture, *Cathartes aura*

KITES, HAWKS, AND FALCONS

—— —— —— —— Mississippi Kite(S), *Ictinia mississippiensis*

—— —— —— —— Northern Harrier, *Circus cyaneus*

—— —— —— —— Red-tailed Hawk, *Buteo jamaicensis*

—— —— —— —— American Kestrel, *Falco sparverius*

PARTRIDGES, GROUSE, TURKEYS, AND QUAIL	♂	♀	JUV.	IMM.
Gray Partridge(NW), *Perdix perdix*	—	—		
Ring-necked Pheasant(N), *Phasianus colchicus*	—	—		
Greater Prairie-Chicken(NW), *Tympanuchus cupido*	—	—		
Northern Bobwhite, *Colinus virginianus*	—	—		

SHOREBIRDS				
Killdeer, *Charadrius vociferus*	—	—		
Upland Sandpiper(N), *Bartramia longicauda*	—	—		
Common Snipe(N), *Gallinago gallinago*	—	—	—	—

♂	♀	JUV.	IMM.	PIGEONS AND DOVES
——	——	——	——	Rock Dove, *Columba livia*
——	——	——	——	Mourning Dove, *Zenaida macroura*
——	——	——	——	Common Ground-Dove(S), *Columbina passerina*

OWLS, GOATSUCKERS, AND SWIFTS

——	——	——	——	Common Barn-Owl, *Tyto alba*
——	——	——	——	Short-eared Owl(N), *Asio flammeus*
——	——	——	——	Common Nighthawk, *Chordeiles minor*
——	——	——	——	Chimney Swift, *Chaetura pelagica*

WOODPECKERS

——	——	——	——	Northern Flicker, *Colaptes auratus*

FLYCATCHERS

——	——	——	——	Alder Flycatcher, *Empidonax alnorum*
——	——	——	——	Willow Flycatcher(N), *Empidonax traillii*
——	——	——	——	Scissor-tailed Flycatcher, *Tyrannus forficatus*

LARKS AND SWALLOWS

——	——	——	——	Horned Lark, *Eremophila alpestris*
——	——	——	——	Tree Swallow(N), *Tachycineta bicolor*

	♂	♀	JUV.	IMM.

Northern Rough-winged Swallow, *Stegidopteryx ruficollis* ___ ___ ___ ___

Bank Swallow, *Riparia riparia* ___ ___ ___ ___

Cliff Swallow, *Hirundo pyrrhonota* ___ ___ ___ ___

Barn Swallow, *Hirundo rustica* ___ ___ ___ ___

CROWS AND WRENS

American Crow, *Corvus brachyrhynchos* ___ ___ ___ ___

Bewick's Wren, *Thryomanes bewickii* ___ ___ ___ ___

Sedge Wren, *Cistothorus platensis* ___ ___ ___ ___

THRUSHES AND MOCKINGBIRDS

American Robin, *Turdus migratorius* ___ ___ ___ ___

Northern Mockingbird, *Mimus polyglottos* ___ ___ ___ ___

SHRIKES AND STARLINGS

Loggerhead Shrike, *Lanius ludovicianus* ___ ___ ___ ___

European Starling, *Sturnis vulgarus* ___ ___ ___ ___

WARBLERS

Blue-winged Warbler, *Vermivora pinus* ___ ___ ___ ___

Yellow Warbler, *Dendroica petechia* ___ ___ ___ ___

Palm Warbler(N), *Dendroica palmarum* ___ ___ ___ ___

♂	♀	JUV.	IMM.	
—	—	—	—	Common Yellowthroat, *Geothlypis trichas*
—	—	—	—	Yellow-breasted Chat, *Icteria virens*

GROSBEAKS, SPARROWS, AND BUNTINGS

♂	♀	JUV.	IMM.	
—	—	—	—	Indigo Bunting, *Passerina cyanea*
—	—	—	—	Dickcissel(W), *Spiza americana*
—	—	—	—	Cassin's Sparrow, *Aimophila cassinii*
—	—	—	—	Chipping Sparrow, *Spizella passerina*
—	—	—	—	Clay-colored Sparrow(NW), *Spizella pallida*
—	—	—	—	Field Sparrow, *Spizella pusilla*
—	—	—	—	Vesper Sparrow, *Pooecetes gramineus*
—	—	—	—	Lark Bunting(NW), *Calamospiza melanocorys*
—	—	—	—	Savannah Sparrow(N), *Passerculus sandwichensis*
—	—	—	—	Grasshopper Sparrow, *Ammodramus savannarum*
—	—	—	—	Henslow's Sparrow(N), *Ammodramus henslowii*
—	—	—	—	LeConte's Sparrow(NW), *Ammodramus leconteii*
—	—	—	—	Sharp-tailed Sparrow(N), *Ammodramus caudacutus*

MEADOWLARKS, BLACKBIRDS, AND ORIOLES	♂	♀	JUV.	IMM.
Bobolink(N), *Dolichonyx oryzivorus*	—	—	—	—
Red-winged Blackbird, *Agelaius phoeniceus*	—	—	—	—
Eastern Meadowlark, *Sturnella magna*	—	—	—	—
Western Meadowlark(W), *Sturnella neglecta*	—	—	—	—
Brewer's Blackbird(NW), *Euphagus cyanocephalus*	—	—	—	—
Boat-tailed Grackle(S), *Quiscalus major*	—	—	—	—
Common Grackle, *Quiscalus quiscula*	—	—	—	—
Brown-headed Cowbird, *Molothrus ater*	—	—	—	—

FINCHES AND ALLIES

	♂	♀	JUV.	IMM.
House Finch, *Carpodacus mexicanus*	—	—	—	—
American Goldfinch(N), *Carduelis tristis*	—	—	—	—
House Sparrow, *Passer domesticus*	—	—	—	—

COMMENTS AND SIGHTING NOTES

. . . .

The Spring Weekend Warbler Watch

DATE

. . . .

PLACE

. . . .

SPECIES
SIGHTED

. . . .

NUMBER

SIGHTINGS OF WOOD WARBLERS

Subfamily Parulinae *(by Genus)*

♂	♀	JUV.	IMM.	GENUS *Vermivora*
——	——	——	——	Blue-winged Warbler, *Vermivora pinus*
——	——	——	——	Golden-winged Warbler (N), *Vermivora chrysoptera*
——	——	——	——	Tennessee Warbler (N), *Vermivora peregrina*
——	——	——	——	Nashville Warbler, *Vermivora ruficapilla*
				GENUS *Parula*
——	——	——	——	Northern Parula, *Parula americana*

GENUS *Dendroica*	♂	♀	JUV.	IMM.
Yellow Warbler, *Dendroica petechia*	——	——	——	——
Chestnut-sided Warbler (N), *Dendroica pensylvanica*	——	——	——	——
Magnolia Warbler, *Dendroica magnolia*	——	——	——	——
Black-throated Blue Warbler (N), *Dendroica caerulescens*	——	——	——	——
Yellow-rumped Warbler (N), *Dendroica coronata*	——	——	——	——
Black-throated Green Warbler (N), *Dendroica virens*	——	——	——	——
Blackburnian Warbler (N), *Dendroica fusca*	——	——	——	——
Yellow-throated Warbler (S), *Dendroica dominica*	——	——	——	——
Pine Warbler, *Dendroica pinus*	——	——	——	——
Prairie Warbler, *Dendroica discolor*	——	——	——	——
Palm Warbler (N), *Dendroica palmarum*	——	——	——	——
Bay-breasted Warbler (N), *Dendroica castanea*	——	——	——	——
Blackpoll Warbler, *Dendroica striata*	——	——	——	——

COMMENTS AND SIGHTING NOTES

. . . .

♂	♀	JUV.	IMM.	**GENUS** *Mniotilta*
___	___	___	___	Black-and-white Warbler, *Mniotilta varia*

GENUS *Setophaga*

___	___	___	___	American Redstart, *Setophaga ruticilla*

GENUS *Protonotaria*

___	___	___	___	Protonotary Warbler, *Protonotaria citrea*

GENUS *Seiurus*

___	___	___	___	Ovenbird, *Seiurus aurocapillus*
___	___	___	___	Northern Waterthrush, *Seiurus noveboracensis*
___	___	___	___	Louisiana Waterthrush, *Seiurus motacilla*

GENUS *Oporornis*

___	___	___	___	Kentucky Warbler (S), *Oporornis formosus*
___	___	___	___	Mourning Warbler, *Oporornis philadelphia*

GENUS *Geothlypis*	♂	♀	JUV.	IMM.
Common Yellowthroat, *Geothlypis trichas*	—	—	—	—
GENUS *Wilsonia*				
Hooded Warbler, *Wilsonia citrina*	—	—	—	—
Wilson's Warbler (N), *Wilsonia pusilla*	—	—	—	—
Canada Warbler (N), *Wilsonia canadensis*	—	—	—	—
GENUS *Icteria*				
Yellow-breasted Chat, *Icteria virens*	—	—	—	—

Year List of Birds in Flight

♂, ♀, JUV., or IMM.	SPECIES	SIGHTED (DATE)	AT (PLACE)

SPECIES SIGHTED (DATE)		AT (PLACE)	♂, ♀, JUV., or IMM.

The Fall Weekend Warbler Watch

DATE

. . . .

PLACE

. . . .

SPECIES SIGHTED

. . . .

N U M B E R

SIGHTINGS OF WOOD WARBLERS

Subfamily Parulinae *(by Genus)*

♂ ♀ JUV. IMM. GENUS *Vermivora*

—— —— —— —— Tennessee Warbler (N), *Vermivora peregrina*

—— —— —— —— Nashville Warbler, *Vermivora ruficapilla*

GENUS *Parula*

—— —— —— —— Northern Parula, *Parula americana*

GENUS *Dendroica*

—— —— —— —— Yellow Warbler, *Dendroica petechia*

—— —— —— —— Chestnut-sided Warbler, *Dendroica pensylvanica*

—— —— —— —— Magnolia Warbler, *Dendroica magnolia*

—— —— —— —— Black-throated Blue Warbler, *Dendroica caerulescens*

—— —— —— —— Yellow-rumped Warbler, *Dendroica coronata*

	♂	♀	JUV.	IMM.

Black-throated Green Warbler, *Dendroica virens* ___ ___ ___ ___

Yellow-throated Warbler, *Dendroica dominica* ___ ___ ___ ___

Pine Warbler, *Dendroica pinus* ___ ___ ___ ___

Prairie Warbler, *Dendroica discolor* ___ ___ ___ ___

Palm Warbler, *Dendroica palmarum* ___ ___ ___ ___

Blackpoll Warbler, *Dendroica striata* ___ ___ ___ ___

GENUS *Mniotilta*

Black-and-white Warbler, *Mniotilta varia* ___ ___ ___ ___

GENUS *Setophaga*

American Redstart, *Setophaga ruticilla* ___ ___ ___ ___

GENUS *Seiurus*

Ovenbird, *Seiurus aurocapillus* ___ ___ ___ ___

Northern Waterthrush, *Seiurus noveboracensis* ___ ___ ___ ___

Louisiana Waterthrush, *Seiurus motacilla* ___ ___ ___ ___

GENUS *Geothlypis*

Common Yellowthroat, *Geothlypis trichas* ___ ___ ___ ___

GENUS *Wilsonia*

Wilson's Warbler (N), *Wilsonia pusilla* ___ ___ ___ ___

Canada Warbler (N), *Wilsonia canadensis* ___ ___ ___ ___

GENUS *Icteria*

Yellow-breasted Chat, *Icteria virens* ___ ___ ___ ___

Wintering Birds

BEGINNING ON

. . . .

D   A   T   E

**AND
ENDING ON**

. . . .

D   A   T   E

AT

. . . .

P L A C E

LOONS, GREBES, AND CORMORANTS

___ Red-throated Loon (N), *Gavia stellata*

___ Common Loon (N), *Gavia immer*

___ Horned Grebe, *Podiceps auritus*

___ Red-necked Grebe, *Podiceps grisegena*

___ Great Cormorant (N), *Phalacrocorax carbo*

HERONS AND IBISES

___ Great Blue Heron, *Ardea herodias*

___ Great Egret (S), *Casmerodius albus*

___ Snowy Egret (S), *Egretta thula*

___ Black-crowned Night-Heron (S), *Nycticorax nycticorax*

___ Glossy Ibis (S), *Plegadis falcinellus*

GEESE AND DUCKS

___ Tundra Swan, *Cygnus columbianus*

___ Snow Goose (S), *Chen caerulescens*

___ Brant, *Branta bernicla*

___ Common Eider, *Somateria mollissima*

___ Harlequin Duck (N), *Histrionicus histrionicus*

___ Oldsquaw (N), *Clangula hyemalis*

___ Black Scoter, *Melanitta nigra*

Surf Scoter, *Melanitta perspicillata* ___

White-winged Scoter, *Melanitta fusca* ___

Common Goldeneye, *Bucephala clangula* ___

Barrow's Goldeneye(N), *Bucephala islandica* ___

Red-breasted Merganser, *Mergus serrator* ___

HAWKS

Rough-legged Hawk, *Buteo lagopus* ___

RAILS

Virginia Rail(S), *Rallus limicola* ___

Sora(S), *Porzana carolina* ___

PLOVERS AND OYSTERCATCHERS

___ Black-bellied Plover, *Pluvialis squatarola*

___ Wilson's Plover (SE), *Charadrius wilsonia*

___ Piping Plover, *Charadrius melodus*

___ Killdeer, *Charadrius vociferus*

___ American Oystercatcher, *Haematopus palliatus*

SANDPIPERS AND ALLIES

___ Greater Yellowlegs (S), *Tringa melanoleuca*

___ Lesser Yellowlegs (S), *Tringa flavipes*

___ Willet (S), *Catoptrophorus semipalmatus*

___ Spotted Sandpiper (S), *Actitis macularia*

___ Marbled Godwit (S), *Limosa fedoa*

___ Ruddy Turnstone, *Arenaria interpres*

___ Red Knot, *Calidris canutus*

___ Semipalmated Sandpiper (S), *Calidris pusilla*

___ Western Sandpiper (S), *Calidris mauri*

___ Least Sandpiper (S), *Calidris minutilla*

___ Purple Sandpiper (N,S), *Calidris maritima*

___ Dunlin (N,S), *Calidris alpina*

___ Common Snipe, *Gallinago gallinago*

___ American Woodcock (S), *Scolopax minor*

GULLS AND TERNS

___ Laughing Gull (S), *Larus atricilla*

___ Ring-billed Gull, *Larus delawarensis*

___ Herring Gull, *Larus argentatus*

___ Iceland Gull (N), *Larus glaucoides*

___ Great Black-backed Gull, *Larus marinus*

Royal Tern(S), *Sterna maxima*   ____

Common Tern(S), *Sterna hirundo*   ____

Forster's Tern(S), *Sterna forsteri*   ____

Black Skimmer(S), *Rynchops niger*   ____

PIGEONS AND DOVES

Rock Dove, *Columba livia*   ____

Mourning Dove, *Zenaida macroura*   ____

OWLS

Common Barn-Owl, *Tyto alba*   ____

Eastern Screech-Owl, *Otus asio*   ____

Great Horned Owl, *Bubo virginianus*   ____

Barred Owl, *Strix varia*   ____

Long-eared Owl, *Asio otus*   ____

Short-eared Owl, *Asio flammeus*   ____

Northern Saw-whet Owl, *Aegolius acadicus*   ____

KINGFISHERS, WOODPECKERS, AND ALLIES

Belted Kingfisher, *Ceryle alcyon*   ____

Red-headed Woodpecker(S), *Melanerpes erythrocephalus*   ____

Red-bellied Woodpecker, *Melanerpes carolinus*   ____

Yellow-bellied Sapsucker, *Sphyrapicus varius*   ____

Downy Woodpecker, *Picoides pubescens*   ____

Hairy Woodpecker, *Picoides villosus*   ____

Red-cockaded Woodpecker(S), *Picoides borealis*   ____

Northern Flicker, *Colaptes auratus*   ____

Pileated Woodpecker, *Dryocopus pileatus*   ____

FLYCATCHERS, LARKS, AND SWALLOWS

___ Eastern Phoebe(S), *Sayornis phoebe*

___ Horned Lark, *Eremophila alpestris*

___ Tree Swallow(S), *Tachycineta bicolor*

JAYS AND CROWS

___ Blue Jay, *Cyanocitta cristata*

___ American Crow, *Corvus brachyrhynchos*

___ Fish Crow(S), *Corvus ossifragus*

CHICKADEES AND TITMICE

___ Black-capped Chickadee, *Parus atricapillus*

___ Carolina Chickadee(S), *Parus carolinensis*

NUTHATCHES

___ Red-breasted Nuthatch, *Sitta canadensis*

___ White-breasted Nuthatch, *Sitta carolinensis*

___ Brown-headed Nuthatch(S), *Sitta pusilla*

CREEPERS AND WRENS

___ Brown Creeper, *Certhia americana*

___ Carolina Wren, *Thryothorus ludovicianus*

___ Bewick's Wren, *Thryomanes bewickii*

___ House Wren(S), *Troglodytes aedon*

___ Winter Wren, *Troglodytes troglodytes*

___ Sedge Wren, *Cistothorus platensis*

___ Marsh Wren(S), *Cistothorus palustris*

KINGLETS AND GNATCATCHERS

Golden-crowned Kinglet, *Regulus satrapa* ____

Ruby-crowned Kinglet(S), *Regulus calendula* ____

Blue-gray Gnatcatcher(S), *Polioptila caerulea* ____

THRUSHES

Eastern Bluebird, *Sialia sialis* ____

Hermit Thrush, *Catharus guttatus* ____

American Robin, *Turdus migratorius* ____

MOCKINGBIRDS AND PIPITS

Gray Catbird(S), *Dumetella carolinensis* ____

Northern Mockingbird, *Mimus polyglottos* ____

Water Pipit, *Anthus spinoletta* ____

WAXWINGS, SHRIKES, STARLINGS, AND VIREOS

Cedar Waxwing, *Bombycilla cedrorum* ____

Northern Shrike(N), *Lanius excubitor* ____

Loggerhead Shrike(S), *Lanius ludovicianus* ____

European Starling, *Sturnus vulgaris* ____

Solitary Vireo(S), *Vireo solitarius* ____

WARBLERS

Orange-crowned Warbler, *Vermivora celata* ____

Yellow-rumped Warbler(N), *Dendroica coronata* ____

Yellow-throated Warbler(S), *Dendroica dominica* ____

Ovenbird(S), *Seiurus aurocapillus* ____

Common Yellowthroat(S), *Geothlypis trichas* ____

TOWHEES, SPARROWS, AND ALLIES

___ Rufous-sided Towhee, *Pipilo erythrophthalmus*

___ Bachman's Sparrow(S), *Aimophila aestivalis*

___ American Tree Sparrow, *Spizella arborea*

___ Chipping Sparrow(S), *Spizella passerina*

___ Field Sparrow, *Spizella pusilla*

___ Lark Sparrow(S), *Chondestes grammacus*

___ Savannah Sparrow, *Passerculus sandwichensis*

___ Grasshopper Sparrow(S), *Ammodramus savannarum*

___ Henslow's Sparrow(S), *Ammodramus henslowii*

___ LeConte's Sparrow(S), *Ammodramus leconteii*

___ Sharp-tailed Sparrow, *Ammodramus caudacutus*

___ Seaside Sparrow, *Ammodramus maritimus*

___ Song Sparrow, *Melospiza melodia*

___ Lincoln's Sparrow(S), *Melospiza lincolnii*

___ Swamp Sparrow, *Melospiza georgiana*

___ White-throated Sparrow, *Zonotrichia albicollis*

___ White-crowned Sparrow(S), *Zonotrichia leucophrys*

___ Harris' Sparrow(W), *Zonotrichia querula*

___ Dark-eyed Junco, *Junco hyemalis*

___ Lapland Longspur, *Calcarius lapponicus*

___ Smith's Longspur, *Calcarius pictus*

___ Chestnut-collared Longspur, *Calcarius ornatus*

___ Snow Bunting, *Plectrophenax nivalis*

MEADOWLARKS, BLACKBIRDS, AND ORIOLES

Red-winged Blackbird, *Agelaius phoeniceus* ___

. . . .

Eastern Meadowlark, *Sturnella magna* ___

Western Meadowlark, *Sturnella neglecta* ___

Rusty Blackbird, *Euphagus carolinus* ___

Brewer's Blackbird (S), *Euphagus cyanocephalus* ___

Common Grackle, *Quiscalus quiscula* ___

Brown-headed Cowbird, *Molothrus ater* ___

Northern Oriole (S), *Icterus galbula* ___

FINCHES AND ALLIES

Pine Grosbeak (N), *Pinicola enucleator* ___

Purple Finch (N), *Carpodacus purpureus* ___

House Finch, *Carpodacus mexicanus* ___

Red Crossbill (N), *Loxia curvirostra* ___

Common Redpoll, *Carduelis flammea* ___

Pine Siskin (N), *Carduelis pinus* ___

American Goldfinch, *Carduelis tristis* ___

Evening Grosbeak, *Coccothraustes verpertinus* ___

Canadian Border and Mountain Birds

DATE

. . . .

PLACE

. . . .

SPECIES SIGHTED

. . . .

NUMBER

SPECIES SIGHTED

♂   ♀   JUV.   IMM.   H A W K S

___ ___ ___ ___ Northern Goshawk, *Accipiter gentilis*

G R O U S E

___ ___ ___ ___ Spruce Grouse, *Dendragapus canadensis*

P U F F I N S

___ ___ ___ ___ Atlantic Puffin, *Fratercula arctica*

O W L S	♂	♀	JUV.	IMM.
Northern Hawk-Owl (Wi), *Surnia ulula*	___	___	___	___
Great Gray Owl (Wi), *Strix nebulosa*	___	___	___	___
Boreal Owl (Wi), *Aegolius funereus*	___	___	___	___

W O O D P E C K E R S A N D A L L I E S

Yellow-bellied Sapsucker (Su), *Sphyrapicus varius*	___	___	___	___
Three-toed Woodpecker, *Picoides tridactylus*	___	___	___	___
Black-backed Woodpecker, *Picoides arcticus*	___	___	___	___

♂	♀	JUV.	IMM.	**FLYCATCHERS**
___	___	___	___	Olive-sided Flycatcher (Su), *Mionectes olivaceus*
___	___	___	___	Yellow-bellied Flycatcher (Su), *Empidonax flaviventris*

JAYS AND CROWS

♂	♀	JUV.	IMM.	
___	___	___	___	Gray Jay, *Perisoreus canadensis*
___	___	___	___	Common Raven, *Corvus corax*

CHICKADEES AND WRENS

___	___	___	___	Boreal Chickadee, *Parus hudsonicus*
___	___	___	___	Winter Wren (Su), *Troglodytes troglodytes*

KINGLETS AND THRUSHES

___	___	___	___	Golden-crowned Kinglet (Su), *Regulus satrapa*
___	___	___	___	Ruby-crowned Kinglet (Su), *Regulus calendula*
___	___	___	___	Gray-cheeked Thrush (Su), *Catharus minimus*
___	___	___	___	Swainson's Thrush (Su), *Catharus ustulatus*
___	___	___	___	Hermit Thrush, *Catharus guttatus*

VIREOS

___	___	___	___	Solitary Vireo (Su), *Vireo solitarius*
___	___	___	___	Philadelphia Vireo (Su), *Vireo philadelphicus*

WARBLERS	♂	♀	JUV.	IMM.
Tennessee Warbler (Su), *Vermivora peregrina*	___	___	___	___
Nashville Warbler (Su), *Vermivora ruficapilla*	___	___	___	___
Magnolia Warbler (Su), *Dendroica magnolia*	___	___	___	___
Cape May Warbler (Su), *Dendroica tigrina*	___	___	___	___
Yellow-rumped Warbler (Su), *Dendroica coronata*	___	___	___	___
Blackburnian Warbler (Su), *Dendroica fusca*	___	___	___	___
Bay-breasted Warbler (Su), *Dendroica castanea*	___	___	___	___
Blackpoll Warbler (Su), *Dendroica striata*	___	___	___	___
Northern Waterthrush (Su), *Seiurus noveboracensis*	___	___	___	___
Mourning Warbler (Su), *Oporonis philadelphia*	___	___	___	___
Wilson's Warbler (Su), *Wilsonia pusilla*	___	___	___	___
Canada Warbler (Su), *Wilsonia canadensis*	___	___	___	___

COMMENTS AND SIGHTING NOTES

. . . .

SPARROWS AND ALLIES

	♂	♀	JUV.	IMM.
LeConte's Sparrow (Su), *Ammodramus leconteii*	___	___	___	___
Lincoln's Sparrow (Su), *Melospiza lincolnii*	___	___	___	___
White-throated Sparrow (Su), *Zonotrichia albicollis*	___	___	___	___
Dark-eyed Junco, *Junco hyemalis*	___	___	___	___

Permanent Residents

BEGINNING ON

. . . .
D   A   T   E

**AND
ENDING ON**

. . . .
D   A   T   E

FOR

. . . .
Y   E   A   R

AT

. . . .
P   L   A   C   E

S P E C I E S   S I G H T E D

(Fill in ♂, ♀, Juv., or Imm.)

P E L I C A N S   A N D   D A R T E R S
_____ Brown Pelican(SE), *Pelecanus occidentalis*
_____ Anhinga(S), *Anhinga anhinga*

H E R O N S ,   I B I S E S ,
A N D   S T O R K S
_____ Great Blue Heron, *Ardea herodias*
_____ Tricolored Heron(SE), *Egretta tricolor*
_____ Yellow-crowned Night Heron(S), *Nycticorax violaceus*
_____ White Ibis(SE), *Eudocimus albus*
_____ Wood Stork(SE), *Mycteria americana*

S W A N S ,   G E E S E ,
A N D   D U C K S
_____ Mute Swan(N), *Cygnus olor*
_____ Canada Goose(N), *Branta canadensis*
_____ American Black Duck(N), *Anas rubripes*
_____ Mallard, *Anas platyrhynchos*

KITES AND HAWKS

Swallow-tailed Kite(SE), *Elanoides forficatus*　——————

Red-tailed Hawk, *Buteo jamaicensis*　——————

American Kestrel, *Falco sparverius*　——————

PARTRIDGES, GROUSE, TURKEYS, AND QUAIL

Gray Partridge(NW), *Perdix perdix*　——————

Ring-necked Pheasant(N), *Phasianus colchicus*　——————

Spruce Grouse(N), *Dendragapus canadensis*　——————

Ruffed Grouse(N), *Bonasa umbellus*　——————

Greater Prairie-Chicken(NW), *Tympanuchus cupido*　——————

Wild Turkey(S), *Meleagris gallopavo*　——————

Northern Bobwhite, *Colinus virginianus*　——————

RAILS, GALLINULES, AND LIMPKINS

Clapper Rail, *Rallus longirostris*　——————

Purple Gallinule(S), *Porphyrula martinica*　——————

Limpkin(S), *Aramus guarauna*　——————

PLOVERS AND GULLS

Killdeer, *Charadrius vociferus*　——————

American Oystercatcher, *Haematopus palliatus*　——————

Great Black-backed Gull(N), *Larus marinus*　——————

PIGEONS AND DOVES

Rock Dove, *Columba livia*　——————

Mourning Dove, *Zenaida macroura*　——————

Common Ground-Dove(S), *Columbina passerina*　——————

O W L S

_____ Eastern Screech-Owl, *Otus asio*

_____ Great Horned Owl, *Bubo virginianus*

_____ Barred Owl, *Strix varia*

_____ Long-eared Owl(N), *Asio otus*

_____ Short-eared Owl(N), *Asio flammeus*

_____ Northern Saw-whet Owl(N), *Aegolius acadicus*

W O O D P E C K E R S

_____ Red-bellied Woodpecker, *Melanerpes carolinus*

_____ Downy Woodpecker, *Picoides pubescens*

_____ Hairy Woodpecker, *Picoides villosus*

_____ Red-cockaded Woodpecker(S), *Picoides borealis*

_____ Three-toed Woodpecker(N), *Picoides tridactylus*

_____ Black-backed Woodpecker(N), *Picoides arcticus*

_____ Pileated Woodpecker, *Dryocopus pileatus*

J A Y S   A N D   C R O W S

_____ Gray Jay(N), *Perisoreus canadensis*

_____ Blue Jay, *Cyanocitta cristata*

_____ Scrub Jay(S), *Aphelocoma coerulescens*

_____ American Crow, *Corvus brachyrhynchos*

_____ Fish Crow, *Corvus ossifragus*

_____ Common Raven(N), *Corvus corax*

C H I C K A D E E S

_____ Black-capped Chickadee(N), *Parus atricapillus*

_____ Carolina Chickadee(S), *Parus carolinensis*

_____ Boreal Chickadee(N), *Parus hudsonicus*

NUTHATCHES, CREEPERS, AND WRENS

Brown-headed Nuthatch, *Sitta pusilla*   _____

Brown Creeper, *Certhia americana*   _____

Carolina Wren, *Thryothorus ludovicianus*   _____

House Wren, *Troglodytes aedon*   _____

MOCKINGBIRDS

Northern Mockingbird, *Mimus polyglottos*   _____

STARLINGS

European Starling, *Sturnus vulgarus*   _____

CARDINALS

Northern Cardinal, *Cardinalis cardinalis*   _____

SPARROWS

Song Sparrow, *Melospiza melodia*   _____

BLACKBIRDS

Red-winged Blackbird, *Agelaius phoeniceus*   _____

FINCHES AND ALLIES

House Finch, *Carpodacus mexicanus*   _____

House Sparrow, *Passer domesticus*   _____

**Florida
Specialties**

DATE
. . . .

PLACE
. . . .

SPECIES
SIGHTED
. . . .

NUMBER

S P E C I E S   S I G H T E D

(Fill in ♂, ♀, Juv., or Imm.)

R E S I D E N T S

Great Blue Heron (White Phase), *Ardea herodias* _____

Greater Flamingo, *Phoenicopterus ruber* _____

Snail Kite, *Rostrhamus sociabilis* _____

Short-tailed Hawk, *Buteo brachyurus* _____

Crested Caracara, *Polyborus plancus* _____

White-crowned Pigeon, *Columba leucocephala* _____

Mangrove Cuckoo, *Coccyzus minor* _____

Groove-billed Ani, *Crotophaga sulcirostris* _____

Burrowing Owl, *Athene cunicularia* _____

Black-whiskered Vireo, *Vireo altiloquus* _____

Scrub Jay, *Aphelocoma coerulescens* _____

I N T R O D U C E D   S P E C I E S

Canary-winged Parakeet, *Brotogeris versicolurus* _____

Red-whiskered Bulbul, *Pycnonotus jocosus* _____

Spot-breasted Oriole, *Icterus pectoralis* _____

Vagrant
Species

COMMENTS	SPECIES	SIGHTED (DATE)	AT (PLACE)

SPECIES	SIGHTED (DATE)	AT (PLACE)	COMMENTS

Arctic
and Alpine
Birds

DATE

. . . .

PLACE

. . . .

SPECIES SIGHTED	SPECIES SIGHTED

. . . .

N U M B E R

♂	♀	JUV.	IMM.	
___	___	___	___	Common Loon, *Gavia immer*
___	___	___	___	Arctic Loon, *Gavia arctica*
___	___	___	___	Tundra Swan, *Cygnus columbianus*
___	___	___	___	King Eider (N), *Somateria spectabilis*
___	___	___	___	Rough-legged Hawk, *Buteo lagopus*
___	___	___	___	Gyrfalcon (N), *Falco rusticolis*
___	___	___	___	Glaucous Gull, *Larus hyperboreus*

	♂	♀	JUV.	IMM.
Snowy Owl(N), *Nyctea scandiaca*	___	___	___	___
Water Pipit, *Anthus spinoletta*	___	___	___	___
Northern Shrike, *Lanius excubitor*	___	___	___	___
Lapland Longspur, *Calcarius lapponicus*	___	___	___	___
Snow Bunting, *Plectrophenax nivalis*	___	___	___	___
Common Redpoll, *Carduelis flammea*	___	___	___	___

North American Travel List

SPECIES	SIGHTED (DATE)	AT (PLACE)

SPECIES	SIGHTED (DATE)	AT (PLACE)	COMMENTS AND SIGHTING NOTES
			. . . .

SPECIES	SIGHTED (DATE)	AT (PLACE)

SPECIES	SIGHTED (DATE)	AT (PLACE)

COMMENTS AND SIGHTING NOTES

. . . .

The Life List

♂ ♀ Juv. Imm.

LOONS

___ ___ ___ ___ Red-throated Loon, *Gavia stellata*

___ ___ ___ ___ Arctic Loon, *Gavia arctica*

___ ___ ___ ___ Common Loon, *Gavia immer*

GREBES

___ ___ ___ ___ Pied-billed Grebe, *Podilymbus podiceps*

___ ___ ___ ___ Horned Grebe, *Podiceps auritus*

___ ___ ___ ___ Red-necked Grebe, *Podiceps grisegena*

___ ___ ___ ___ Eared Grebe, *Podiceps nigricollis*

___ ___ ___ ___ Western Grebe, *Aechmophorus occidentalis*

SHEARWATERS, PETRELS, GANNETS, AND PELICANS

___ ___ ___ ___ Northern Fulmar, *Fulmarus glacialis*

♂ ♀ Juv. Imm.

___ ___ ___ ___ Cory's Shearwater, *Calonectris diomedea*

___ ___ ___ ___ Greater Shearwater, *Puffinus gravis*

___ ___ ___ ___ Sooty Shearwater, *Puffinus griseus*

___ ___ ___ ___ Manx Shearwater, *Puffinus puffinus*

___ ___ ___ ___ Audubon's Shearwater, *Puffinus lherminieri*

___ ___ ___ ___ Wilson's Storm-Petrel, *Oceanites oceanicus*

___ ___ ___ ___ Leach's Storm-Petrel, *Oceanodroma leucorhoa*

___ ___ ___ ___ Northern Gannet, *Sula bassanus*

___ ___ ___ ___ American White Pelican, *Pelecanus erythrorhynchos*

___ ___ ___ ___ Brown Pelican, *Pelecanus occidentalis*

CORMORANTS, DARTERS, AND FRIGATEBIRDS

♂ ♀ Juv. Imm.

Great Cormorant, *Phalacrocorax carbo* — — — —

Double-crested Cormorant, *Phalacrocorax auritus* — — — —

Olivaceous Cormorant, *Phalacrocorax olivaceus* — — — —

Anhinga, *Anhinga anhinga* — — — —

Magnificent Frigatebird, *Fregata magnificens* — — — —

BITTERNS AND HERONS

American Bittern, *Botaurus lentiginosus* — — — —

Least Bittern, *Ixobrychus exilis* — — — —

Great Blue Heron, *Ardea herodias* — — — —

Great Egret, *Casmerodius albus* — — — —

Snowy Egret, *Egretta thula* — — — —

Little Blue Heron, *Egretta caerulea* — — — —

Tricolored Heron, *Egretta tricolor* — — — —

Reddish Egret, *Egretta rufescens* — — — —

Cattle Egret, *Bubulcus ibis* — — — —

Green-backed Heron, *Butorides striatus* — — — —

Black-crowned Night-Heron, *Nycticorax nycticorax* — — — —

Yellow-crowned Night-Heron, *Nycticorax violaceus* — — — —

IBISES, SPOONBILLS, STORKS, AND FLAMINGOS

White Ibis, *Eudocimus albus* — — — —

Glossy Ibis, *Plegadis falcinellus* — — — —

White-faced Ibis, *Plegadis chihi* — — — —

Roseate Spoonbill, *Ajaia ajaja* — — — —

Wood Stork, *Mycteria americana* — — — —

Greater Flamingo, *Phoenicopterus ruber* — — — —

SWANS, GEESE, AND DUCKS

Fulvous Whistling-Duck, *Dendroygna bicolor* — — — —

Tundra Swan, *Cygnus columbianus* — — — —

Mute Swan, *Cygnus olor* — — — —

♂	♀	Juv.	Imm.	
—	—	—	—	Lesser White-fronted Goose, *Anser erythropus*
—	—	—	—	Greater White-fronted Goose, *Anser albifrons*
—	—	—	—	Snow Goose, *Chen caerulescens*
—	—	—	—	Brant, *Branta bernicla*
—	—	—	—	Canada Goose, *Branta canadensis*
—	—	—	—	Wood Duck, *Aix sponsa*
—	—	—	—	Green-winged Teal, *Anas crecca*
—	—	—	—	American Black Duck, *Anas rubripes*
—	—	—	—	Mallard, *Anas platyrhynchos*
—	—	—	—	Northern Pintail, *Anas acuta*
—	—	—	—	Blue-winged Teal, *Anas discors*
—	—	—	—	Northern Shoveler, *Anas clypeata*
—	—	—	—	Gadwall, *Anas strepera*
—	—	—	—	Eurasian Wigeon, *Anas penelope*
—	—	—	—	American Wigeon, *Anas americana*
—	—	—	—	Canvasback, *Aythya valisineria*
—	—	—	—	Redhead, *Aythya americana*
—	—	—	—	Ring-necked Duck, *Aythya collaris*

♂	♀	Juv.	Imm.	
—	—	—	—	Greater Scaup, *Aythya marila*
—	—	—	—	Lesser Scaup, *Aythya affinis*
—	—	—	—	Common Eider, *Somateria mollissima*
—	—	—	—	King Eider, *Somateria spectabilis*
—	—	—	—	Harlequin Duck, *Histrionicus histrionicus*
—	—	—	—	Oldsquaw, *Clangula hyemalis*
—	—	—	—	Black Scoter, *Melanitta nigra*
—	—	—	—	Surf Scoter, *Melanitta perspicillata*
—	—	—	—	White-winged Scoter, *Melanitta fusca*
—	—	—	—	Common Goldeneye, *Bucephala clangula*
—	—	—	—	Barrow's Goldeneye, *Bucephala islandica*
—	—	—	—	Bufflehead, *Bucephala albeola*
—	—	—	—	Hooded Merganser, *Lophodytes cucullatus*
—	—	—	—	Common Merganser, *Mergus merganser*
—	—	—	—	Red-breasted Merganser, *Mergus serrator*

	♂	♀	Juv.	Imm.

Ruddy Duck, *Oxyura jamaicensis* ___ ___ ___ ___

VULTURES

Black Vulture, *Coragyps atratus* ___ ___ ___ ___

Turkey Vulture, *Cathartes aura* ___ ___ ___ ___

KITES, EAGLES, HAWKS, AND ALLIES

Osprey, *Pandion haliaetus* ___ ___ ___ ___

American Swallow-tailed Kite, *Elanoides forficatus* ___ ___ ___ ___

Snail Kite, *Rostrhamus sociabilis* ___ ___ ___ ___

Mississippi Kite, *Ictinia mississippiensis* ___ ___ ___ ___

Bald Eagle, *Haliaeetus leucocephalus* ___ ___ ___ ___

Northern Harrier, *Circus cyaneus* ___ ___ ___ ___

Sharp-shinned Hawk, *Accipiter striatus* ___ ___ ___ ___

Cooper's Hawk, *Accipiter cooperii* ___ ___ ___ ___

Northern Goshawk, *Accipiter gentilis* ___ ___ ___ ___

Red-shouldered Hawk, *Buteo lineatus* ___ ___ ___ ___

	♂	♀	Juv.	Imm.

Broad-winged Hawk, *Buteo platypterus* ___ ___ ___ ___

Short-tailed Hawk, *Buteo brachyurus* ___ ___ ___ ___

Swainson's Hawk, *Buteo swainsoni* ___ ___ ___ ___

Red-tailed Hawk, *Buteo jamaicensis* ___ ___ ___ ___

Ferruginous Hawk, *Buteo regalis* ___ ___ ___ ___

Rough-legged Hawk, *Buteo lagopus* ___ ___ ___ ___

Golden Eagle, *Aquila chrysaetos* ___ ___ ___ ___

CARACARAS AND FALCONS

Crested Caracara, *Polyborus plancus* ___ ___ ___ ___

American Kestrel, *Falco sparverius* ___ ___ ___ ___

Merlin, *Falco columbarius* ___ ___ ___ ___

Peregrine Falcon, *Falco peregrinus* ___ ___ ___ ___

Gyrfalcon, *Falco rusticolus* ___ ___ ___ ___

PARTRIDGES, GROUSE, TURKEYS, AND QUAIL

Gray Partridge, *Perdix perdix* ___ ___ ___ ___

Ring-necked Pheasant, *Phasianus colchicus* ___ ___ ___ ___

♂	♀	Juv.	Imm.	
		___	___	Spruce Grouse, *Dendragapus canadensis*
___	___	___	___	Willow Ptarmigan, *Lagopus lagopus*
___	___	___	___	Rock Ptarmigan, *Lagopus mutus*
___	___	___	___	Ruffed Grouse, *Bonasa umbellus*
___	___	___	___	Greater Prairie-Chicken, *Tympanuchus cupido*
				Lesser Prairie-Chicken, *Tympanuchus pallidicinctus*
___	___	___	___	Sharp-tailed Grouse, *Tympanuchus phasianellus*
___	___	___	___	Wild Turkey, *Meleagris gallopavo*
___	___	___	___	Northern Bobwhite, *Colinus virginianus*

RAILS, GALLINULES, COOTS, AND LIMPKINS

♂	♀	Juv.	Imm.	
___	___	___	___	Yellow Rail, *Coturnicops noveboracensis*
___	___	___	___	Black Rail, *Laterallus jamaicensis*
___	___	___	___	Clapper Rail, *Rallus longirostris*
___	___	___	___	King Rail, *Rallus elegans*

♂	♀	Juv.	Imm.	
___	___	___	___	Virginia Rail, *Rallus limicola*
___	___	___	___	Sora, *Porzana carolina*
___	___	___	___	Purple Gallinule, *Porphyrula martinica*
___	___	___	___	Common Moorhen, *Gallinula chloropus*
___	___	___	___	American Coot, *Fulica americana*
___	___	___	___	Limpkin, *Aramus guarauna*

CRANES, PLOVERS, AND OYSTERCATCHERS

♂	♀	Juv.	Imm.	
___	___	___	___	Sandhill Crane, *Grus canadensis*
___	___	___	___	Whooping Crane, *Grus americana*
___	___	___	___	Black-bellied Plover, *Pluvialis squatarola*
___	___	___	___	Lesser Golden-Plover, *Pluvialis apricaria*
___	___	___	___	Wilson's Plover, *Charadrius wilsonia*
___	___	___	___	Semipalmated Plover, *Charadrius semipalmatus*
___	___	___	___	Piping Plover, *Charadrius melodus*
___	___	___	___	Killdeer, *Charadrius vociferus*

American Oystercatcher, *Haematopus palliatus* ♂ ♀ Juv. Imm. _ _ _ _

STILTS, AVOCETS, SANDPIPERS, PHALAROPES, AND ALLIES

Black-necked Stilt, *Himantopus mexicanus* _ _ _ _

American Avocet, *Recurvirostra americana* _ _ _ _

Greater Yellowlegs, *Tringa melanoleuca* _ _ _ _

Lesser Yellowlegs, *Tringa flavipes* _ _ _ _

Solitary Sandpiper, *Tringa solitaria* _ _ _ _

Willet, *Catoptrophorus semipalmatus* _ _ _ _

Spotted Sandpiper, *Actitis macularia* _ _ _ _

Upland Sandpiper, *Bartramia longicauda* _ _ _ _

Whimbrel, *Numenius phaeopus* _ _ _ _

Long-billed Curlew, *Numenius americanus* _ _ _ _

Hudsonian Godwit, *Limosa haemastica* _ _ _ _

Marbled Godwit, *Limosa fedoa* _ _ _ _

Ruddy Turnstone, *Arenaria interpres* ♂ ♀ Juv. Imm.

Red Knot, *Calidris canutus*

Sanderling, *Calidris alba* _ _ _ _

Semipalmated Sandpiper, *Calidris pusilla*

Western Sandpiper, *Calidris mauri*

Least Sandpiper, *Calidris minutilla*

White-rumped Sandpiper, *Calidris fuscicollis*

Baird's Sandpiper, *Calidris bairdii* _ _ _ _

Pectoral Sandpiper, *Calidris melanotos*

Purple Sandpiper, *Calidris maritima*

Dunlin, *Calidris alpina*

Curlew Sandpiper, *Calidris ferruginea* _ _ _ _

Stilt Sandpiper, *Calidris himantopus*

Buff-breasted Sandpiper, *Tryngites subruficollis* _ _ _ _

Short-billed Dowitcher, *Limnodromus griseus*

Long-billed Dowitcher, *Limnodromus scolopaceus* _ _ _ _

♂	♀	Juv.	Imm.	
_	_	_	_	Common Snipe, *Gallinago gallinago*
_	_	_	_	American Woodcock, *Scolopax minor*
_	_	_	_	Wilson's Phalarope, *Phalaropus tricolor*
_	_	_	_	Red-necked Phalarope, *Phalaropus lobatus*
_	_	_	_	Red Phalarope, *Phalaropus fulicaria*

SKUAS, GULLS, TERNS, AND SKIMMERS

♂	♀	Juv.	Imm.	
_	_	_	_	Pomarine Jaeger, *Stercorarius pomarinus*
_	_	_	_	Parasitic Jaeger, *Stercorarius parasiticus*
_	_	_	_	Long-tailed Jaeger, *Stercorarius longicaudus*
_	_	_	_	Laughing Gull, *Larus artricilla*
_	_	_	_	Franklin's Gull, *Larus pipixcan*
_	_	_	_	Little Gull, *Larus minutus*
_	_	_	_	Common Black-headed Gull, *Larus ridibundus*
_	_	_	_	Bonaparte's Gull, *Larus philadelphia*
_	_	_	_	Ring-billed Gull, *Larus delawarensis*
_	_	_	_	Herring Gull, *Larus argentatus*

♂	♀	Juv.	Imm.	
_	_	_	_	Thayer's Gull, *Larus thayeri*
_	_	_	_	Iceland Gull, *Larus glaucoides*
_	_	_	_	Lesser Black-backed Gull, *Larus fuscus*
_	_	_	_	Glaucous Gull, *Larus hyperboreus*
_	_	_	_	Great Black-backed Gull, *Larus marinus*
_	_	_	_	Black-legged Kittiwake, *Rissa tridactyla*
_	_	_	_	Sabine's Gull, *Xema sabini*
_	_	_	_	Ivory Gull, *Pagophila eburnea*
_	_	_	_	Gull-billed Tern, *Sterna nilotica*
_	_	_	_	Caspian Tern, *Sterna caspia*
_	_	_	_	Royal Tern, *Sterna maxima*
_	_	_	_	Sandwich Tern, *Sterna sandvicensis*
_	_	_	_	Roseate Tern, *Sterna dougallii*
_	_	_	_	Common Tern, *Sterna hirundo*
_	_	_	_	Arctic Tern, *Sterna paradisaea*
_	_	_	_	Forster's Tern, *Sterna forsteri*
_	_	_	_	Least Tern, *Sterna antillarum*
_	_	_	_	Black Tern, *Chlidonias niger*

Black Skimmer,
Rynchops niger

	♂	♀	Juv.	Imm.

AUKS, MURRES, AND PUFFINS

Dovekie, *Alle alle* — — — —

Common Murre, — — — —
Uria aalge

Thick-billed Murre, — — — —
Uria lomvia

Razorbill, *Alca* — — — —
torda

Black Guillemot, — — — —
Cepphus grylle

Atlantic Puffin, — — — —
Fratercula arctica

PIGEONS AND DOVES

Rock Dove, — — — —
Columba livia

White-crowned — — — —
Pigeon, *Columba leucocephala*

Mourning Dove, — — — —
Zenaida macroura

Common Ground- — — — —
Dove, *Columbina passerina*

CUCKOOS AND ROADRUNNERS

Black-billed — — — —
Cuckoo, *Coccyzus erythropthalmus*

Yellow-billed — — — —
Cuckoo, *Coccyzus americanus*

Mangrove Cuckoo, — — — —
Coccyzus minor

Greater Roadrunner, — — — —
Geococcyx californianus

OWLS

Common Barn-Owl, — — — —
Tyto alba

Eastern Screech- — — — —
Owl, *Otus asio*

Great Horned Owl, — — — —
Bubo virginianus

Snowy Owl, *Nyctea* — — — —
scandiaca

Northern Hawk- — — — —
Owl, *Surnia ulula*

Burrowing Owl, — — — —
Athene cunicularia

Barred Owl, *Strix* — — — —
varia

Great Gray Owl, — — — —
Strix nebulosa

Long-eared Owl, — — — —
Asio otus

Short-eared Owl, — — — —
Asio flammeus

Boreal Owl, — — — —
Aegolius funereus

Northern Saw-whet — — — —
Owl, *Aegolius acadicus*

GOATSUCKERS AND ALLIES

Common — — — —
Nighthawk,
Chordeiles minor

♂	♀	Juv.	Imm.	
___	___	___	___	Common Poorwill, *Phalaenoptilus nuttallii*
___	___	___	___	Chuck-will's-widow, *Caprimulgus carolinensis*
___	___	___	___	Whip-poor-will, *Caprimulgus vociferus*

SWIFTS AND HUMMINGBIRDS

♂	♀	Juv.	Imm.	
___	___	___	___	Chimney Swift, *Chaetura pelagica*
___	___	___	___	White-throated Swift, *Aeronautes saxatalis*
___	___	___	___	Ruby-throated Hummingbird, *Archilochus colubris*
___	___	___	___	Broad-tailed Hummingbird, *Selasphorus platycercus*

KINGFISHERS, WOODPECKERS, AND ALLIES

♂	♀	Juv.	Imm.	
___	___	___	___	Belted Kingfisher, *Ceryle alcyon*
___	___	___	___	Lewis' Woodpecker, *Melanerpes lewis*
___	___	___	___	Red-headed Woodpecker, *Melanerpes erythrocephalus*
___	___	___	___	Red-bellied Woodpecker, *Melanerpes carolinus*

♂	♀	Juv.	Imm.	
___	___	___	___	Yellow-bellied Sapsucker, *Sphyrapicus varius*
___	___	___	___	Downy Woodpecker, *Picoides pubescens*
___	___	___	___	Hairy Woodpecker, *Picoides villosus*
___	___	___	___	Red-cockaded Woodpecker, *Picoides borealis*
___	___	___	___	Three-toed Woodpecker, *Picoides tridactylus*
___	___	___	___	Black-backed Woodpecker, *Picoides arcticus*
___	___	___	___	Northern Flicker, *Colaptes auratus*
___	___	___	___	Pileated Woodpecker, *Dryocopus pileatus*

FLYCATCHERS

♂	♀	Juv.	Imm.	
___	___	___	___	Olive-sided Flycatcher, *Mionectes olivaceus*
___	___	___	___	Western Wood-Pewee, *Contopus sordidulus*
___	___	___	___	Eastern Wood-Pewee, *Contopus virens*
___	___	___	___	Yellow-bellied Flycatcher, *Empidonax flaviventris*
___	___	___	___	Acadian Flycatcher, *Empidonax virescens*

	♂	♀	Juv.	Imm.
Alder Flycatcher, *Empidonax alnorum*	—	—	—	—
Willow Flycatcher, *Empidonax traillii*	—	—	—	—
Least Flycatcher, *Empidonax minimus*	—	—	—	—
Dusky Flycatcher, *Empidonax oberholseri*	—	—	—	—
Western Flycatcher, *Empidonax difficilis*	—	—	—	—
Eastern Phoebe, *Sayornis phoebe*	—	—	—	—
Say's Phoebe, *Sayornis saya*	—	—	—	—
Dusky-capped Flycatcher, *Myiarchus tuberculifer*	—	—	—	—
Great Crested Flycatcher, *Myiarchus crinitus*	—	—	—	—
Cassin's Kingbird, *Tyrannus vociferans*	—	—	—	—
Western Kingbird, *Tyrannus verticalis*	—	—	—	—
Eastern Kingbird, *Tyrannus tyrannus*	—	—	—	—
Gray Kingbird, *Tyrannus dominicensis*	—	—	—	—
Scissor-tailed Flycatcher, *Tyrannus forficatus*	—	—	—	—

LARKS AND SWALLOWS

	♂	♀	Juv.	Imm.
Horned Lark, *Eremophila alpestris*	—	—	—	—
Purple Martin, *Progne subis*	—	—	—	—
Tree Swallow, *Tachycineta bicolor*	—	—	—	—
Northern Rough-winged Swallow, *Stelgidopteryx ruficollis*	—	—	—	—
Bank Swallow, *Riparia riparia*	—	—	—	—
Cliff Swallow, *Hirundo pyrrhonota*	—	—	—	—
Barn Swallow, *Hirundo rustica*	—	—	—	—

JAYS, MAGPIES, AND CROWS

	♂	♀	Juv.	Imm.
Gray Jay, *Perisoreus canadensis*	—	—	—	—
Steller's Jay, *Cyanocitta stelleri*	—	—	—	—
Blue Jay, *Cyanocitta cristata*	—	—	—	—
Scrub Jay, *Aphelocoma coerulescens*	—	—	—	—
Pinyon Jay, *Gymnorhinus cyanocephalus*	—	—	—	—
Clark's Nutcracker, *Nucifraga columbiana*	—	—	—	—

♂	♀	Juv.	Imm.	
				Black-billed Magpie, *Pica pica*
—	—	—	—	American Crow, *Corvus brachyrhynchos*
—	—	—	—	Fish Crow, *Corvus ossifragus*
—	—	—	—	Common Raven, *Corvus corax*

CHICKADEES AND TITMICE

♂	♀	Juv.	Imm.	
—	—	—	—	Black-capped Chickadee, *Parus atricapillus*
—	—	—	—	Carolina Chickadee, *Parus carolinensis*
—	—	—	—	Boreal Chickadee, *Parus hudsonicus*
—	—	—	—	Tufted Titmouse, *Parus bicolor*

NUTHATCHES, CREEPERS, WRENS, AND DIPPERS

♂	♀	Juv.	Imm.	
—	—	—	—	Red-breasted Nuthatch, *Sitta canadensis*
—	—	—	—	White-breasted Nuthatch, *Sitta carolinensis*
—	—	—	—	Brown-headed Nuthatch, *Sitta pusilla*
—	—	—	—	Brown Creeper, *Certhia americana*
—	—	—	—	Rock Wren, *Salpinctes obsoletus*

♂	♀	Juv.	Imm.	
				Canyon Wren, *Catherpes mexicanus*
—	—	—	—	Carolina Wren, *Thryothorus ludovicianus*
—	—	—	—	Bewick's Wren, *Thryomanes bewickii*
—	—	—	—	House Wren, *Troglodytes aedon*
—	—	—	—	Winter Wren, *Troglodytes troglodytes*
—	—	—	—	Sedge Wren, *Cistothorus platensis*
—	—	—	—	Marsh Wren, *Cistothorus palustris*
—	—	—	—	American Dipper, *Cinclus mexicanus*

KINGLETS, GNATCATCHERS, THRUSHES, AND ALLIES

♂	♀	Juv.	Imm.	
—	—	—	—	Golden-crowned Kinglet, *Regulus satrapa*
—	—	—	—	Ruby-crowned Kinglet, *Regulus calendula*
—	—	—	—	Blue-gray Gnatcatcher, *Polioptila caerulea*
—	—	—	—	Northern Wheatear, *Oenanthe oenanthe*
—	—	—	—	Eastern Bluebird, *Sialia sialis*

	♂	♀	Juv.	Imm.
Mountain Bluebird, *Sialia currucoides*	—	—	—	—
Townsend's Solitaire, *Myadestes townsendi*	—	—	—	—
Veery, *Catharus fuscescens*	—	—	—	—
Gray-cheeked Thrush, *Catharus minimus*	—	—	—	—
Swainson's Thrush, *Catharus ustulatus*	—	—	—	—
Hermit Thrush, *Catharus guttatus*	—	—	—	—
Wood Thrush, *Hylocichla mustelina*	—	—	—	—
American Robin, *Turdus migratorius*	—	—	—	—

MOCKINGBIRDS, THRASHERS, AND PIPITS

	♂	♀	Juv.	Imm.
Gray Catbird, *Dumetella carolinensis*	—	—	—	—
Northern Mockingbird, *Mimus polyglottos*	—	—	—	—
Brown Thrasher, *Toxostoma rufum*	—	—	—	—
Water Pipit, *Anthus spinoletta*	—	—	—	—

WAXWINGS, SHRIKES, STARLINGS, AND VIREOS

	♂	♀	Juv.	Imm.
Bohemian Waxwing, *Bombycilla garrulus*	—	—	—	—
Cedar Waxwing, *Bombycilla cedrorum*	—	—	—	—
Northern Shrike, *Lanius excubitor*	—	—	—	—
Loggerhead Shrike, *Lanius ludovicianus*	—	—	—	—
European Starling, *Sturnus vulgaris*	—	—	—	—
White-eyed Vireo, *Vireo griseus*	—	—	—	—
Bell's Vireo, *Vireo bellii*	—	—	—	—
Solitary Vireo, *Vireo solitarius*	—	—	—	—
Yellow-throated Vireo, *Vireo flavifrons*	—	—	—	—
Warbling Vireo, *Vireo gilvus*	—	—	—	—
Philadelphia Vireo, *Vireo philadelphicus*	—	—	—	—
Red-eyed Vireo, *Vireo olivaceus*	—	—	—	—

WARBLERS

	♂	♀	Juv.	Imm.
Bachman's Warbler, *Vermivora bachmanii*	—	—	—	—
Blue-winged Warbler, *Vermivora pinus*	—	—	—	—

♂	♀	Juv.	Imm.	
—	—	—	—	Golden-winged Warbler, *Vermivora chrysoptera*
—	—	—	—	Tennessee Warbler, *Vermivora peregrina*
—	—	—	—	Orange-crowned Warbler, *Vermivora celata*
—	—	—	—	Nashville Warbler, *Vermivora ruficapilla*
—	—	—	—	Northern Parula, *Parula americana*
—	—	—	—	Yellow Warbler, *Dendroica petechia*
—	—	—	—	Chestnut-sided Warbler, *Dendroica pensylvanica*
—	—	—	—	Magnolia Warbler, *Dendroica magnolia*
—	—	—	—	Cape May Warbler, *Dendroica tigrina*
—	—	—	—	Black-throated Blue Warbler, *Dendroica caerulescens*
—	—	—	—	Yellow-rumped Warbler, *Dendroica coronata*
—	—	—	—	Black-throated Green Warbler, *Dendroica virens*
—	—	—	—	Blackburnian Warbler, *Dendroica fusca*
—	—	—	—	Yellow-throated Warbler, *Dendroica dominica*
—	—	—	—	Pine Warbler, *Dendroica pinus*

♂	♀	Juv.	Imm.	
—	—	—	—	Kirtland's Warbler, *Dendroica kirtlandii*
—	—	—	—	Prairie Warbler, *Dendroica discolor*
—	—	—	—	Palm Warbler, *Dendroica palmarum*
—	—	—	—	Bay-breasted Warbler, *Dendroica castanea*
—	—	—	—	Blackpoll Warbler, *Dendroica striata*
—	—	—	—	Cerulean Warbler, *Dendroica cerulea*
—	—	—	—	Black-and-white Warbler, *Mniotilta varia*
—	—	—	—	American Redstart, *Setophaga ruticilla*
—	—	—	—	Prothonotary Warbler, *Protonotaria citrea*
—	—	—	—	Worm-eating Warbler, *Helmitheros vermivorus*
—	—	—	—	Swainson's Warbler, *Limnothlypis swainsonii*
—	—	—	—	Ovenbird, *Seiurus aurocapillus*
—	—	—	—	Northern Waterthrush, *Seiurus noveboracensis*
—	—	—	—	Louisiana Waterthrush, *Seiurus motacilla*
—	—	—	—	Kentucky Warbler, *Oporornis formosus*

	♂	♀	Juv.	Imm.

Connecticut Warbler, *Oporornis agilis*

Mourning Warbler, *Oporornis philadelphia* — — — —

Common Yellowthroat, *Geothlypis trichas* — — — —

Hooded Warbler, *Wilsonia citrina* — — — —

Wilson's Warbler, *Wilsonia pusilla* — — — —

Canada Warbler, *Wilsonia canadensis* — — — —

Yellow-breasted Chat, *Icteria virens* — — — —

TANAGERS

Summer Tanager, *Piranga rubra* — — — —

Scarlet Tanager, *Piranga olivacea* — — — —

Western Tanager, *Piranga ludoviciana* — — — —

CARDINALS AND GROSBEAKS

Northern Cardinal, *Cardinalis cardinalis* — — — —

Rose-breasted Grosbeak, *Pheucticus ludovicianus* — — — —

Black-headed Grosbeak, *Pheucticus melanocephalus* — — — —

Blue Grosbeak, *Guiraca caerulea*

Lazuli Bunting, *Passerina amoena* — — — —

Indigo Bunting, *Passerina cyanea* — — — —

Painted Bunting, *Passerina ciris* — — — —

Dickcissel, *Spiza americana* — — — —

TOWHEES, SPARROWS, AND ALLIES

Green-tailed Towhee, *Pipilo chlorurus* — — — —

Rufous-sided Towhee, *Pipilo erythrophthalmus* — — — —

Bachman's Sparrow, *Aimophila aestivalis* — — — —

Cassin's Sparrow, *Aimophila cassinii* — — — —

Rufous-crowned Sparrow, *Aimophila ruficeps* — — — —

American Tree Sparrow, *Spizella arborea* — — — —

Chipping Sparrow, *Spizella passerina* — — — —

Clay-colored Sparrow, *Spizella pallida* — — — —

Field Sparrow, *Spizella pusilla* — — — —

Vesper Sparrow, *Pooecetes gramineus* — — — —

| | | | Lark Sparrow, *Chondestes grammacus* |

____ Black-throated Sparrow, *Amphispiza bilineata*

____ Lark Bunting, *Calamospiza melanocorys*

____ Savannah Sparrow, *Passerculus sandwichensis*

____ Baird's Sparrow, *Ammodramus bairdii*

____ Grasshopper Sparrow, *Ammodramus savannarum*

____ Henslow's Sparrow, *Ammodramus henslowii*

____ LeConte's Sparrow, *Ammodramus leconteii*

____ Sharp-tailed Sparrow, *Ammodramus caudacutus*

____ Seaside Sparrow, *Ammodramus maritimus*

____ Fox Sparrow, *Passerella iliaca*

____ Song Sparrow, *Melospiza melodia*

____ Lincoln's Sparrow, *Melospiza lincolnii*

____ Swamp Sparrow, *Melospiza georgiana*

____ White-throated Sparrow, *Zonotrichia albicollis*

____ White-crowned Sparrow, *Zonotrichia leucophrys*

____ Harris' Sparrow, *Zonotrichia querula*

____ Dark-eyed Junco, *Junco hyemalis*

____ McCown's Longspur, *Calcarius mccownii*

____ Lapland Longspur, *Calcarius lapponicus*

____ Smith's Longspur, *Calcarius pictus*

____ Chestnut-collared Longspur, *Calcarius ornatus*

____ Snow Bunting, *Plectrophenax nivalis*

MEADOWLARKS, BLACKBIRDS, AND ORIOLES

____ Bobolink, *Dolichonyx oryzivorus*

____ Red-winged Blackbird, *Agelaius phoeniceus*

____ Eastern Meadowlark, *Sturnella magna*

	♂	♀	Juv.	Imm.
Western Meadowlark, *Sturnella neglecta*	—	—	—	—
Yellow-headed Blackbird, *Xanthocephalus xanthocephalus*	—	—	—	—
Rusty Blackbird, *Euphagus carolinus*	—	—	—	—
Brewer's Blackbird, *Euphagus cyanocephalus*	—	—	—	—
Great-tailed Grackle, *Quiscalus mexicanus*	—	—	—	—
Boat-tailed Grackle, *Quiscalus major*	—	—	—	—
Common Grackle, *Quiscalus quiscula*	—	—	—	—
Brown-headed Cowbird, *Molothrus ater*	—	—	—	—
Orchard Oriole, *Icterus spurius*	—	—	—	—
Northern Oriole, *Icterus galbula*	—	—	—	—

FINCHES AND ALLIES

	♂	♀	Juv.	Imm.
Rosy Finch, *Leucosticte arctoa*	—	—	—	—
Pine Grosbeak, *Pinicola enucleator*	—	—	—	—
Purple Finch, *Carpodacus purpureus*	—	—	—	—
House Finch, *Carpodacus mexicanus*	—	—	—	—

	♂	♀	Juv.	Imm.
Red Crossbill, *Loxia curvirostra*	—	—	—	—
White-winged Crossbill, *Loxia leucoptera*	—	—	—	—
Common Redpoll, *Carduelis flammea*	—	—	—	—
Hoary Redpoll, *Carduelis hornemanni*	—	—	—	—
Pine Siskin, *Carduelis pinus*	—	—	—	—
Lesser Goldfinch, *Carduelis psaltria*	—	—	—	—
American Goldfinch, *Carduelis tristis*	—	—	—	—
Evening Grosbeak, *Coccothraustes verpertinus*	—	—	—	—
House Sparrow, *Passer domesticus*	—	—	—	—

The
Maps

Following are selected geographic range maps for some of the more commonly seen species of the region. Included here are maps showing distribution for breeding, wintering, and resident ranges. No range map can be entirely definitive, and those included here provide *general parameters* of geographic ranges for selected species. The maps indicate the activities of various species only east of the 100th meridian in North America.

Resident species are defined as those that are nonmigratory, regularly residing in a given area. The distribution of the migratory species is described as either "breeding" or "wintering," in that the bird is usually in one or the other locale during the year. However, some migratory birds do have resident ranges, usually in the area between the breeding and wintering ranges. In order to keep these maps concise, some resident ranges for migrants have not been included. In some cases, the species may be in the same locale both when it is breeding and wintering, or the range may overlap.

It is important to remember that a species will be found only in appropriate habitats within its range. Note that our winter is actually summer for visiting seabirds that winter south of the equator.

Colors and patterns are used on these maps to distinguish species and behavior. For the most part, two species are shown on a single map, each species indicated by the use of an individual color. The varying patterns on the maps indicate the different ranges of particular activities, such as breeding, wintering, or resident status, of a bird. A wintering range is shown by the use of a lined pattern, whereas a dot pattern indicates the breeding locale of the species. A tone of the species' color shows resident ranges. Sometimes a third color (purple or orange) may be created. Rather than indicate a third bird's activity, it is indicative of overlapping ranges of activity of two birds. In addition, the order of the maps that follow corresponds to the taxonomic order of bird species.

Range and distribution information is often very useful in making a definitive identification, and should be used in conjunction with other identifying techniques whenever possible. Very often a bird can be eliminated as the one having been assumed to have been sighted because it does not conform to the known range or behaviors of the presumed sighted species.

Maps read left to right; labels read top to bottom

Breeding

Wintering

Resident

Common Loon

Pied-billed Grebe

Double-crested Cormorant

Anhinga

American Bittern

Least Bittern

Green-backed Heron

Black-crowned Night-Heron

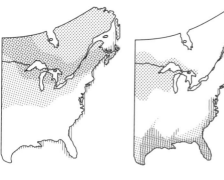

Glossy Ibis ●

Snow Goose ●

Green-winged Teal ●

Blue-winged Teal ●

American Black Duck ●

Gadwall ●

Mallard ●

Northern Harrier ●

Sharp-shinned Hawk ●

Cooper's Hawk ●

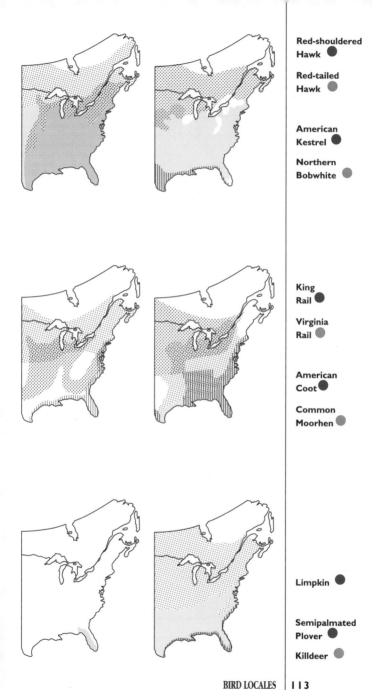

Red-shouldered Hawk ●
Red-tailed Hawk ●

American Kestrel ●
Northern Bobwhite ●

King Rail ●
Virginia Rail ●

American Coot ●
Common Moorhen ●

Limpkin ●

Semipalmated Plover ●
Killdeer ●

Spotted Sandpiper ●

Least Sandpiper ●

American Woodcock ●

Laughing Gull ●

Herring Gull ●

Common Tern ●

Mourning Dove ●

Yellow-billed Cuckoo ●

Common Barn-Owl ●

Eastern Screech-Owl ●

Great Horned Owl ●

Barred Owl ●

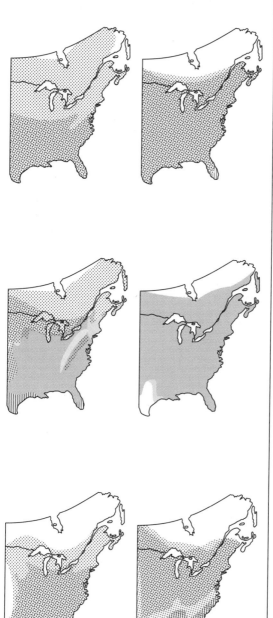

Common Nighthawk ●

Chuck-will's-widow ●

Chimney Swift ●

Ruby-throated Hummingbird ●

Belted Kingfisher ●

Red-headed Woodpecker ●

Downy Woodpecker ●

Hairy Woodpecker ●

Eastern Wood-Pewee ●

Acadian Flycatcher ●

Eastern Phoebe ●

Great Crested Flycatcher ●

Eastern
Kingbird ●

Gray
Kingbird ●

Purple
Martin ●

Tree
Swallow ●

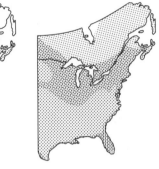

Northern
Rough-winged
Swallow ●

Bank
Swallow ●

Barn
Swallow ●

Blue
Jay ●

Scrub
Jay ●

American
Crow ●

Common
Raven ●

Black-capped
Chickadee ●

Carolina
Chickadee ●

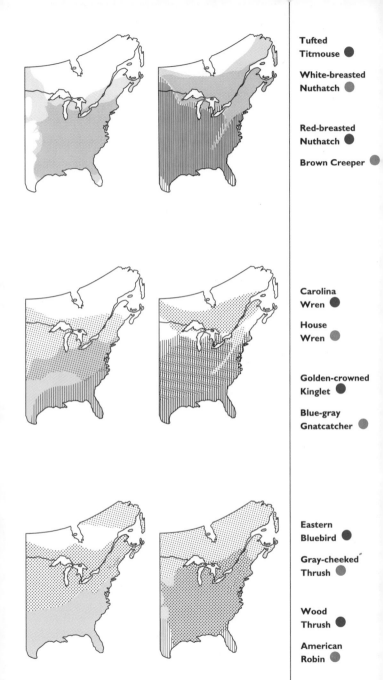

Tufted Titmouse ●

White-breasted Nuthatch ●

Red-breasted Nuthatch ●

Brown Creeper ●

Carolina Wren ●

House Wren ●

Golden-crowned Kinglet ●

Blue-gray Gnatcatcher ●

Eastern Bluebird ●

Gray-cheeked Thrush ●

Wood Thrush ●

American Robin ●

Gray Catbird ●

Northern Mockingbird ●

Brown Thrasher ●

Cedar Waxwing ●

Loggerhead Shrike ●

European Starling ●

White-eyed Vireo ●

Solitary Vireo ●

Yellow-throated Vireo ●

Warbling Vireo ●

Red-eyed Vireo ○

Northern Parula ●

Yellow Warbler ●

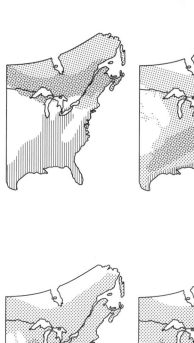

Cape May Warbler ●

Yellow-rumped Warbler ●

Yellow-throated Warbler ●

Black-and-white Warbler ●

American Redstart ●

Prothonotary Warbler ●

Ovenbird ●

Louisiana Waterthrush ●

Mourning Warbler ●

Common Yellowthroat ●

Yellow-breasted Chat ●

Northern Cardinal ●

Scarlet Tanager ●

Rose-breasted Grosbeak ●

Blue Grosbeak ●

Indigo Bunting ●

Dickcissel ●

Rufous-sided Towhee ●

American Tree Sparrow ●

Chipping Sparrow ●

Field Sparrow ●

Vesper Sparrow ●

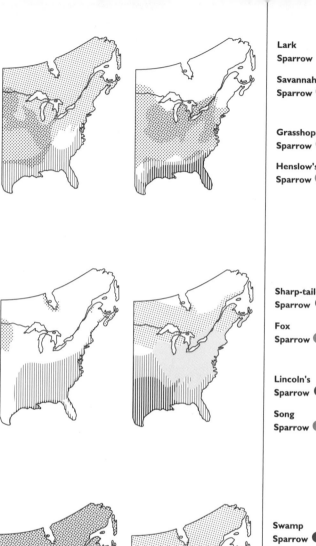

Lark Sparrow ●

Savannah Sparrow ●

Grasshopper Sparrow ●

Henslow's Sparrow ●

Sharp-tailed Sparrow ●

Fox Sparrow ●

Lincoln's Sparrow ●

Song Sparrow ●

Swamp Sparrow ●

White-throated Sparrow ●

White-crowned Sparrow ●

Dark-eyed Junco ●

Red-winged
Blackbird ●

Rusty
Blackbird ●

Brown-headed
Cowbird ●

Orchard
Oriole ●

Northern
(Baltimore)
Oriole ●

Purple
Finch ●

House
Finch ●

Pine
Siskin ●

American
Goldfinch ●

Eastern
Meadowlark ●

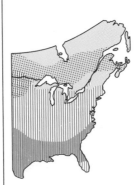

THE MAPS

Competitions

Contact the following organizations for information:

Big Day
American Birding Association
P.O. Box 6599
Colorado Springs, CO 80934
(800) 634-7736

Christmas Bird Count
% C.B.C. Editor
American Birds
National Audubon Society
950 Third Avenue
New York, NY 10022
(212) 832-3200

The World Series of Birding
% Mr. Peter Dunne
Scherman Hoffman
   Sanctuary
New Jersey Audubon Society
P.O. Box 693
Bernardsville, NJ 07924
(908) 766-5787

Audubon, Ornithological, and Naturalist Societies

UNITED STATES

. . . .

N A T I O N A L

American Birding Association
P.O. Box 6599
Colorado Springs, CO 80934
(800) 634-7736

American Ornithologists Union
% National Museum of
   Natural History
Smithsonian Institution
10th and Constitution Avenue
   Northwest
Washington, D.C. 20560
(202) 357-2051

Association of Field Ornithologists
P.O. Box 21618
Columbus, OH 43221

International Council for Bird Preservation
1250 24th Street
   Northeast
Washington, D.C. 20037
(202) 778-9563

National Audubon Society
950 Third Avenue
New York, NY 10022
(212) 832-3200

. . . .

S   T   A   T   E

Contact these societies for local chapters:

Connecticut Audubon Society
2325 Burr Street
Fairfield, CT 06430
(203) 259–6305

Florida Audubon Society
1101 Audubon Way
Maitland, FL 32651
(305) 647–2615

Hawaii Audubon Society
P.O. Box 22832
Honolulu, HI 96822

Illinois Audubon Society
P.O. Box 608
Wayne, IL 60184
(312) 584–6290

Indiana Audubon Society
Mary Gray Bird Sanctuary
RR6
Connersville, IN 47331
(317) 825–9788

Maine Audubon Society
Gilsland Farm
118 Route 1
Falmouth, ME 04105
(207) 781–2330

**Massachusetts Audubon
Society, Inc.**
South Great Road
Lincoln, MA 01773
(617) 259–9500

Michigan Audubon Society
409 West E. Avenue
Kalamazoo, MI 49007
(616) 344–8648

**Audubon Society of New
Hampshire**
3 Silk Farm Road
P.O. Box 528B
Concord, NH 03301
(603) 244–9909

**New Jersey Audubon
Society**
790 Ewing Avenue
P.O. Box 125
Franklin Lake, NJ 07417
(201) 891–1211

**Audubon Society of Rhode
Island**
40 Bowen Street
Providence, RI 02903
(401) 521–1670

C A N A D A

. . . .

N A T I O N A L

**Canadian Wildlife
Federation**
2740 Queensview Drive
Ottawa, Ontario
K2B 1A2
(613) 721-2286

**Federation of Ontario
Naturalists**
355 Lesmill Road
Don Mills, Ontario
M3B 2W8
(416) 444-8419

**Federation of B.C.
Naturalists**
Room 321
1367 West Broadway
Vancouver, B.C.
V6H 4A9
(604) 737-3057

**Canadian Nature
Federation/Bookshop**
453 Sussex Drive
Ottawa, Ontario
K1N 6Z4
(613) 238-6154

Canadian Wildlife Service
351 St. Joseph's Blvd.
17th Floor, P. V. M.
Hull, Quebec
K1A 0H3
(819) 997-1301
(Ontario Head Office)
(819) 953-1412
(Publications Department)

Periodicals

Audubon
National Audubon Society
950 Third Avenue
New York, NY 10022
(212) 832-3200
*bimonthly publication free
   with membership*

The Auk
American Ornithologists
   Union
% National Museum of
   Natural History
Smithsonian Institution
10th and Constitution Avenue
   Northwest
Washington, D.C. 20560
(202) 357-2051

Birding
American Birding Association
P.O. Box 4335
Austin, TX 78765
(512) 474-4804
bimonthly

The Living Bird
Quarterly
Laboratory of Ornithology at
   Cornell University
159 Sapsucker Woods Road
Ithaca, NY 14850
(607) 255-7317
free with membership

. . . .

CANADA

*These publications cover all
aspects of wildlife
preservation*

The Canadian Field
Naturalist
Ottawa Field Naturalists Club

Box 3264
Postal Station C
Ottawa, ON KIY 4J5
(613) 722-3050

Nature Canada
Canada Nature Federation
75 Albert Street
Ottawa, ON K1P 6G1
(613) 238-6154

Seasons
Federation of Ontario
Naturalists
355 Lesmill Road
Don Mills, ON M3B 2W8
(416) 444-8419

Books

*The A.O.U. Check-list of
North American Birds,* 6th
ed. Lawrence, Kans.: Allen
Press Inc., 1983.

Farrand, John, ed. *The
Audubon Society Master
Guide to Birding.* 3 vols.
New York: Knopf, 1984.

*National Geographic
Society's Field Guide to the
Birds of North America.*
Washington, D.C.: National
Geographic Society, 1983.

Peterson, Roger Tory. *A Field
Guide to the Birds East of
the Rockies,* 4th ed. Boston:
Houghton Mifflin Co., 1980.

_____ . *A Field Guide to
Western Birds,* 2d ed.
Boston: Houghton Mifflin Co.,
1961.

Robbins, Chandler S., et al.
Birds of North America, rev.
ed. Racine, Wis.: Western
Publishers, 1983.